DATE DUE

DEMCO 38-297

Readings in Literary Criticism 15
CRITICS ON EZRA POUND

Readings in Literary Criticism

CRITICS ON
EZRA POUND

Readings in Literary Criticism
Edited by E. San Juan, Jr.

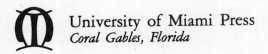
University of Miami Press
Coral Gables, Florida

CONTENTS

ACKNOWLEDGMENTS

John Berryman: from "The Poetry of Ezra Pound," *Partisan Review,* vol. 16, April 1949. Copyright © 1949 by *Partisan Review.* Reprinted by permission of the author and the publisher.

R. P. Blackmur: from *Language as Gesture.* Copyright 1946 by Richard P. Blackmur. Reprinted by permission of Harcourt Brace Jovanovich, Inc.

Hayden Carruth: from "Ezra Pound and the Great Style," *Saturday Review,* April 9, 1966. Copyright 1966 by Saturday Review, Inc. Reprinted by permission of the author and the publisher.

Donald Davie: from *Ezra Pound: Poet as Sculptor.* Copyright © 1964 by Donald Davie. Reprinted by permission of Oxford University Press, Inc.

George Dekker: from *Sailing After Knowledge: The Cantos of Ezra Pound.* Copyright 1963 by Routledge and Kegan Paul, Ltd. Reprinted by permission of the publisher.

Richard Eberhart: from *Quarterly Review of Literature,* vol. 5, 1949. Copyright © 1949 by the *Quarterly Review of Literature.* Reprinted by permission of the publisher.

Hugh Kenner: from "The Broken Mirrors and the Mirror of Memory" in *Motive and Method in the Cantos of Ezra Pound.* Copyright © 1954 by Hugh Kenner. Reprinted by permission of Columbia University Press.

Robert Langbaum: from *The Poetry of Experience.* Copyright © 1957 by Random House, Inc. Reprinted by permission of the publisher.

Wyndham Lewis: from *Time and Western Man.* Copyright © 1927 by Chatto and Windus, London; first Beacon Paperback edition published in 1957 by arrangement with Methuen and Co., Ltd. Reprinted by permission of Beacon Press.

N. Christoph De Nagy: from *Ezra Pound's Poetics and Literary Tradition.* Copyright 1966 by Franke Verlag, Bern. Reprinted by permission of the publisher.

Paul A. Olson: from *Thought,* vol. 35, 1960. Copyright © 1960 by *Thought.* Reprinted by permission of the publisher.

Roy Harvey Pearce: from *The Continuity of American Poetry.* Copyright © 1961 by Princeton University Press; Princeton paperback, 1965. Reprinted by permission of Princeton University Press.

Forrest Read: from *The Sewanee Review,* vol. 65, 1957. Copyright 1957 by The University of the South. Reprinted by permission of the publisher.

M. L. Rosenthal: from *The Modern Poets: A Critical Introduction.* Copyright © 1960 by M. L. Rosenthal. Reprinted by permission of Oxford University Press, Inc.

Margaret Schlauch: from *Science and Society,* vol. 13, 1949. Copyright © 1949 by *Science and Society.* Reprinted by permission of the publisher.

Edith Sitwell: from *The Atlantic Book of English and American Poetry.* Copyright © 1958 by Little, Brown and Company. Reprinted by permission of Atlantic-Little, Brown and Company.

Noel Stock: from *Poet in Exile: Ezra Pound.* Copyright © 1964 by Noel Stock. Reprinted by permission of the Manchester University Press.

Allen Tate: from *Essays of Four Decades.* Copyright © 1968 by Allen Tate. Reprinted by permission of The Swallow Press, Inc.

Ray B. West: from *Quarterly Review of Literature,* vol. 5, 1949. Copyright © 1949 by the *Quarterly Review of Literature.* Reprinted by permission of the publisher.

William Carlos Williams: from *Selected Essays of William Carlos Williams.* Copyright 1931 by William Carlos Williams. Reprinted by permission of New Directions Publishing Corporation.

Yvor Winters: from *In Defense of Reason.* Copyright © 1947 by Yvor Winters. Reprinted by permission of The Swallow Press, Inc.

W. B. Yeats: from the Introduction to the *Oxford Book of Modern Verse.* Copyright © 1936 by The Clarendon Press. Reprinted by permission of The Clarendon Press, Oxford.

Louis Zukofsky: from *Prepositions.* Copyright 1967 by Louis Zukofsky. Reprinted by permission of the author and the Horizon Press.

INTRODUCTION

AFTER MORE than twenty years of casebook diagnoses and apologetics, criticism of Ezra Pound's literary achievement and its impact is now characterized by warm objectivity, informed perspective, and experimental latitude. In fact it has become the academic consensus and the avant-garde's view that modern poetry in English is largely Pound's creation. William Carlos Williams, Robert Lowell, Charles Olson, and Allen Ginsberg, among others, confirm this impression. Criticism of Pound's work has likewise acquired discretion and adventuresome reach.

The selection of commentaries, essays, and estimates gathered here illustrates the scope and depth of Pound's accomplishment and the corresponding responses of contemporary poets and critics. This anthology aims chiefly to help the student understand Pound's intentions, the design and meaning of his works, by suggesting a wide-ranging variety of approaches. It would be foolish to start from scratch or from gut-level reflexes.

I assume that most readers of poetry desire to heighten their enjoyment by inquiring into the causes of their aesthetic experience. Correct judgment is based on a proper analysis of the work's intent and its universe of discourse. It requires familiarity with the historical background and the socio-cultural orientation of the work. The end of criticism is a deepened total response of the whole person. Ultimately the value of any critical instrument or apparatus depends on how well it enables us to gain pleasure and intensified global awareness from the experience of reading. This coincides with Pound's own primary motivation in his criticism: "the refreshment, revitalization, and 'making new' of literature in our own time."

T. S. Eliot has suggested that Pound's reputation will eventually rest on his total work for literature, not only his poetry and criticism but also his influence on men and events at a turning point in cultural history. Pound single-handedly instigated the revolutionary transition of English poetry from the Browning-Swinburne stage to the modernist one. Eliot also pointed out that "Pound was original in insisting that poetry is an art, an art which demands the most arduous application and study: and in seeing that in our time it had to be a highly conscious art" (*Poetry*, 1946).

Clarification of terminology and the emphasis on *virtù*, the creative intelligence in action, distinguish Pound's concern as a critic. By his example in theory and practice, we are thus enjoined to exercise subtle tact, open-mindedness, and rigorous discrimination in appreciating the selections in this volume.

For a just evaluation of any criticism, it is important to take into account three determinants regarding the internal character of the critical discourse.

First, we must consider what particular problem or set of problems the critic is engaged in resolving. Second, we must examine how the critic, in confronting his specific problem, formulates a set of assumptions or basic distinctions by means of which he states his problem as a problem of a particular kind and argues to conclusions about it. Third, we must perceive how the critic applies a mode of argument which he thinks suited to his aims on a particular occasion. Anyone who asserts or denies something is surely conditioned by his taste and sensibility, and by his knowledge of pertinent facts. But over and above this, one cannot say anything sensible about the qualities of a given piece of writing unless he entertains some implicit assumptions about the nature of literature and the function of criticism.

The student's task in ascertaining the worth of a critical discourse requires the identification of those determinants. He should seek to define the assumptions of the critic concerning both the literary work he is explaining and the purpose of the critical act. For these assumptions underlie the reason for his asking certain types of questions and finding answers to them. Moreover, he should try to grasp the devices of reasoning by which the answers were established. Any act of reasoning or reflection involves the selection of principles and methods that a problem demands, and conversely the principles or methods chosen determine the limits of the questions asked and the answers obtained.

Applying the above criteria, we will discover three kinds of criticism: (1) technical criticism, which deals with questions of artistic construction, ends and means, differences in various literary species; (2) qualitative criticism, which deals with general qualities of mind or values that distinguish one writer from another, irrespective of species; and (3) circumstantial criticism, which deals not with universal principles but with historical forces that affect the genesis of species or the development of general qualities of mind.[1]

It may not be possible to subject the extracts in this book to this kind of sophisticated analysis. Nonetheless the student should keep in mind the variety of critical interest, methodologies, and languages, so that he will not arrive at naive conclusions unwarranted by the texts.

Ezra Pound himself would strongly endorse this activity of "demarcation," the need for concrete and substantive demonstrations. He proposed that "the function of criticism is to efface itself when it has established its dissociations" (*Make It New*, 1934). He urged the imperative of striving for order by the canon of "excernment," that is, the precise application of word to thing, the congruence of statement to fact, the *mot juste*.

Early in his career Pound expressed the belief that he would violate any convention "that impedes or obscures the determination of the law, or the precise rendering of the impulse" (*Pavannes and Divisions*, 1918). His devotion to an objective cosmos, a Confucian "universe of interacting strains and tensions," compelled him to seek the exact and efficient correlation of particulars.

1. For further elaboration, see R. S. Crane, *The Idea of the Humanities* (Chicago, 1967), Vol. 2, pt. 3.

The classical axioms of lucid notation, economy or condensation, and accuracy Pound combined into an organon of truth whereby he could hold—to echo Yeats's phrase—reality and justice in a single thought.

Pound believed in coherence and harmony in nature, in an objective order behind the dynamic motion of life where things work out their fate. The classic is the always new; art must be in constant flux in order to live. Beauty is "aptness to purpose," reminding us of "what is worth while." Whereas technique is the test of sincerity for Pound, he also maintained that "the what is much more important than how" (*Paris Review*, 1962).

With his belief in the reality of a moral order pervading the universe, Pound espoused an anti-egoistic creed—a disciplined ethos of the producer, a heroic ethics of the maker who would serve as a medium or vehicle for disclosing the relations between things: "The *forma*, the immortal *concetto*, the concept, the dynamic form which is like the rose-pattern driven into the dead iron filings by the magnet" (*Guide to Kulchur*, 1938). Pound expected less humility than integrity: "Every critic should give indication of the sources and limits of his knowledge."

For Pound, the function of criticism inheres in an ideal of refined civilization, in humane learning and urbane taste: "The ignominious failure of ANY critic (however low) is to fail to find something to arouse the appetite of his audience to read, to see, to experience." Unless the artist or critic strictly pursues the quest for clarity, he will most likely lapse into sentimentality and self-indulgence. He will commit fraud in the performance of his métier. "Usura" is Pound's term for any betrayal of commitment to one's calling (see esp. Canto XLV).

Pound established the fundamental premise of his critical and poetic endeavors in the moral convictions embodied in "The Serious Artist" (1913), "How to Read" (1929), and *ABC of Reading* (1934). Two statements epitomize his position: "The social function of the writer is to keep the nation's language living and capable of precise registration"; and "If any human activity is sacred, it is the formulation of thought in clear speech for the use of humanity; any falsification or evasion is evil."

Make It New: this appeal, with all its profound implications, may be said to sum up Pound's critical standard. The poet's education toward this end signifies the mobilizing of knowledge—"ideas going into action"—in which the authority of tradition and the poet's intuitive resources fuse creatively. By "new-minting" speech, the poet sharpens our perceptive faculties and actualizes the whole man in himself and in us. Pound believes in an intelligence working in nature, an entelechy of processes and organisms which the poet seizes in "radiant gists" and articulates by the ideogrammic method. The poet as shaping spirit operates as the master dialectician of the self and the world.

Because Pound's multiform preoccupations defy the efforts of any single critic, the study of his work has always been a collaborative enterprise. Conflicts and disputes naturally arise regarding various aspects of Pound's career. Partisanship may be unavoidable. But it is only fair to take into account the poet's total commitment as evidenced by his whole life work.

The *Cantos*, it is generally agreed, is the most technically brilliant and vitally complex epic of the first half of this century. No one will claim to have fully explicated this massive architectonic feat. Some critics argue that the poem, still in progress, is a huge assembly of fragments lacking an overall design; others contend that it possesses a tight structure, a rationale of its own, which is difficult to grasp at first glance. No doubt its metaphysics and epistemology offer a challenge to future critics.

So far commentaries on the *Cantos* have failed to clearly "demarcate" the nature of the whole composition because most of them begin from the wrong assumption that the poem has a mimetic form, that is, a form whose unity is derived from the action it seeks to represent. Contrary to this view, I suggest that the poem may be better construed as exhibiting a didactic scheme, though it employs mimetic or representational devices. The incidents in the poem are not conceived in a sequential manner (the Odysseus mask/persona is a technique for conveying the quotidian, the durable or recurrent, and the permanent all of which interlock in the Homeric voyage of self-discovery). Rather, the incidents are managed as incidents representing ideas and abstract conceptions.

The *Cantos* exhibits the mode of moral allegory in the broadest sense. It seeks to inculcate a comprehensive doctrine by way of representing actions (as synthesized, for instance, by three leading motifs: *Nekuia* or descent to Hades, Ovidian metamorphosis, historic parallels). Its completion depends not upon the actions but upon the doctrine or set of beliefs.

A just evaluation would then lead us to conceive the strategy of the *Cantos* as founded on the poet's aim of persuading or instructing us about a specific world view. The poet expresses his ideas by using techniques effective and powerful enough in getting us to feel the necessary emotional disposition toward his ideas. He presents his beliefs in the emotional light in which he wants us to accept them. He employs types and methods of proof, whether logical in themselves or consistent to a given frame of mind. These proofs may include narrative material which implies his thesis by induction (exemplum), by deduction (allegory), by analogy (parable, fable), or by other means. Thesis and manner of proof together constitute the argument of the didactic poem.

The argument of the *Cantos* has often been conceived within the framework of a strict mimetic poem, though scholars like Hugh Kenner and Donald Davie have elucidated relevant facets of the ideological system unifying the poem. Perhaps what the Bollingen Committee said in justifying its 1949 award may be considered one major principle of Pound's didacticism, namely, the faith in the validity of "that objective perception of value on which civilized society must rest." Pound's whole career is oriented around this insight into the objective value of humane learning and civilized reason, an insight poignantly voiced in the *Pisan Cantos* (LXXXI):

> To have gathered from the air a live tradition
> or from a fine old eye the unconquered flame
> This is not vanity.

The purpose of this collection is neither to exhibit a formal school of criticism nor to concentrate on a given thematic concern of scholars and critics, but to provide a sampling of the range and variety of the critical responses aroused by Pound's writings. No attempt at comprehensiveness has been made. Within the space limitations, I have tried to represent as many important critics as possible—except T. S. Eliot whose publisher has refused permission to reprint. For recent criticism, see the bibliography.

University of Connecticut, 1972   E. SAN JUAN, JR.

TABLE OF IMPORTANT DATES

1885	Ezra Weston Loomis Pound born October 30 in Hailey, Idaho.
1901-05	Undergraduate at University of Pennsylvania and Hamilton College. Ph. B., Hamilton College, 1905.
1906	M. A. in Romanics, University of Pennsylvania. Travel to Europe as Harrison Fellow in Romanics.
1907	Instructor for a half year in French and Spanish at Wabash College, Crawfordsville, Indiana.
1908	*A Lume Spento,* Pound's first volume of poems, published in Venice. Residence in London until 1920.
1913	*Personae and Exultations.* Principles of Imagist Poetry published in the April issue of *Poetry: A Magazine of Verse.*
1914	Married Dorothy Shakespear. Article "Vorticism" published in *Fortnightly Review.* Contributor to Wyndham Lewis' *Blast* (1914-15).
1919	*Quia Pauper Amavi,* including three "Cantos" and "Homage to Sextus Propertius."
1920	Residence in Paris until 1924. *Hugh Selwyn Mauberley* and *Instigations.*
1921	*Poems, 1918-21,* including Cantos IV-VII.
1925	*A Draft of XVI Cantos.* Settled in Rapallo, Italy.
1926	Omar Shakespear Pound born September 10 in Paris. *Personae: The Collected Poems of Ezra Pound,* exclusive of the Cantos.
1934	*Eleven New Cantos: XXXI-XLI. ABC of Reading. Make It New* published in London (American edition, 1935).
1939	First visit to the United States since 1910. Honorary D. Litt., Hamilton College.
1940	Cantos LII-LXXI. Began radio addresses in Rome as personal propaganda in support of U. S. Constitution, as he claimed.
1943	Indicted *in absentia* for treason by the District Court of the United States for the District of Columbia.
1945	Arrested by U. S. Army in Genoa. Sent to American military prison compound near Pisa; three weeks' solitary confinement in a steel cage. Flown to Washington, D. C., in November to stand trial.
1946	Adjudged insane and remanded to St. Elizabeth's Hospital for the Criminally Insane.
1948	*The Cantos of Ezra Pound,* collected edition including *The Pisan Cantos* (74-84).
1949	Bollingen Award for Poetry (1948) awarded Pound for *The Pisan Cantos.*
1950	*The Letters of Ezra Pound, 1907-1941,* edited by D. D. Paige.
1954	*Literary Essays of Ezra Pound,* with an introduction by T. S. Eliot.
1958	Indictment for treason dismissed in U. S. District Court. Released from St. Elizabeth's. Resides with daughter at the Schloss Brunnenburg, Italy, near Merano.
1959	*Thrones: 96-109 de los Cantares.* Canto CXI completed by Christmas.

1960	*Impact: Essays on the Ignorance and Decline of American Civilization* (ed. by Noel Stock).
1965	Attends funeral of T. S. Eliot at Westminster and visits widow of W. B. Yeats in Dublin—January.
1967	*Selected Cantos of Ezra Pound,* edited with an introduction.
1969	Brief visit to U. S., Hamilton College.
1970	First printing of Cantos I-CXVII in one volume.

W. B. YEATS

Ezra Pound

EZRA POUND has made flux his theme; plot, characterization, logical discourse, seem to him abstractions unsuitable to a man of his generation. He is mid-way in an immense poem in *vers libre* called for the moment *The Cantos,* where the metamorphosis of Dionysus, the descent of Odysseus into Hades, repeat themselves in various disguises, always in association with some third that is not repeated. Hades may become the hell where whatever modern men he most disapproves of suffer damnation, the metamorphosis petty frauds practised by Jews at Gibraltar. The relation of all the elements to one another, repeated or unrepeated, is to become apparent when the whole is finished. There is no transmission through time, we pass without comment from ancient Greece to modern England, from modern England to medieval China; the symphony, the pattern, is timeless, flux eternal and therefore without movement. Like other readers I discover at present merely exquisite or grotesque fragments. He hopes to give the impression that all is living, that there are no edges, no convexities, nothing to check the flow; but can such a poem have a mathematical structure?
. . .

When I consider his work as a whole I find more style than form; at moments more style, more deliberate nobility and the means to convey it than in any contemporary poet known to me, but it is constantly interrupted, broken, twisted into nothing by its direct opposite, nervous obsession, nightmare, stammering confusion; he is an economist, poet, politician, raging at malignants with inexplicable characters and motives, grotesque figures out of a child's book of beasts. This loss of self-control, common among uneducated revolutionists, is rare—Shelley had it in some degree—among men of Ezra Pound's culture and erudition. Style and its opposite can alternate, but form must be full, sphere-like, single. Even where there is no interruption he is often content, if certain verses and lines have style, to leave unbridged transitions, unexplained ejaculations, that make his meaning unintelligible. He has great influence, more perhaps than any contemporary except Eliot, is probably the source of that lack of form and consequent obscurity which is the main defect of Auden, Day Lewis, and their school, a school which, as will presently be seen, I greatly admire. Even where the style is sustained throughout one gets an impression, especially when he is writing in *vers libre,* that he has not got all the wine into the bowl, that he is a brilliant improvisator translating at sight from an unknown Greek masterpiece. . . .

From *The Oxford Book of Modern Verse* (Oxford: Clarendon Press, 1936), pp. xxiv-xxvi.

WYNDHAM LEWIS

A Man in Love with the Past

NOW A kind of mock-bitter, sententious *terseness* characterizes most of Pound's semi-original verse, and even mars some of his translations. And then there is the 'terseness' that enlivens his journalism, which must be distinguished from the other more fundamental 'terseness' to which I am now drawing attention. In his journalism his 'terseness' is of much the same order as Dr. Mann's; it is of a breezy and boisterous order. For example, such violent expressions as 'bunk, junk, spoof, mush, slush, tosh, bosh,' are favourites with him; and he remains convinced that such over-specifically *manly* epithets are universally effective, in spite of all proof to the contrary. But it is not that sort of 'terseness' to which I wished to refer.

The other, more fundamental, 'terseness' of Pound is also of a sententious and, by implication, 'manly' order. It seems to me to make his better personal verse (as distinguished from his translations) very monotonous, and gives it all a rather stupid ring. It is not, of course, the nature of metre chosen to which I am referring, but the melodramatic, chopped, 'bitter' tone suggested by the abrupt clipping and stopping to which he is addicted. It is the laconicism of the strong silent man. Were he a novelist, you would undoubtedly find the description 'He broke off' repeatedly used. In his verse he is always 'breaking off.' And he 'breaks off,' indeed, as a rule, twice in every line.

> Cave of Nerea
> She like a great shell curved.
> And the boat drawn without sound
> Without odour of ship-work,
> Nor bird-cry, nor any noise of wave moving,
> Nor splash of porpoise, nor any noise of wave moving,
> Within her cave, Nerea,
> She like a great shell curved.

That actually seems to belong to the repetitive hypnotic method of Miss Stein and Miss Loos. 'She like a great shell curved,' and the 'any noise of wave moving,' both repeated, are in any case swinburnian stage-properties. The whole passage with its abrupt sententious pauses is unpleasantly reminiscent of the second-rate actor accustomed to take heavy and emotional parts. Perhaps in this next quotation it will be seen better what I mean:—

> Now supine in burrow, half over-arched bramble,

One eye for the sea, through that peek-hole,
Gray light, with Athene.
Zothar, and her elephants, the gold loin-cloth,
The systrum, shaken, shaken,
            the cohort of her dancers.
And Aletha, by bend of the shore,
            with her eyes seaward,
            and in her hands sea-wrack
Salt-bright.

How you are supposed to read this, of course, is with great stops upon—*burrow,
bramble, peek-hole, gray light, Athene, Zothar, elephants, loin-cloth, systrum, shaken,
dancers, Aletha, seaward, sea-wrack, salt-bright.* The way the personnel of the
poem are arranged, sea-wrack in the hand of one, Aletha 'with her eyes
seaward,' the gold loin-cloth of another, etc., makes it all effectively like a
spirited salon-picture, gold framed and romantically 'classical.' It is full of
'sentiment,' as is the Cave of Nerea; it is all made up of well-worn stage-
properties; and it is composed upon a series of histrionic pauses, intended to
be thrilling and probably beautiful.

These extracts are from Cantos XVIII.-XIX., and made their appearance in
the *Q. Review.* Here is a specimen of Pound's more intimate verse (taken from
the same place):—

And the answer to that is: Wa'al he had the ten thousand.
And old Spinder, that put up the 1870 gothick memorial,
He tried to pull me on Marx, and he told me
About the 'romance of his business'; . . . So I sez:
Waal haow is it you're over here, right off the Champz Elyza?
And how can yew be here? Why dont the fellers at home
Take it all off you? . . .
'Oh' he sez 'I ain't had to rent any money . . .
'It's a long time since I had tew rent any money.'

All Pound's comic reliefs speak the same tongue; they are all jocose and
conduct their heavy german-american horseplay in the same personal argot of
Pound. They can never have illumined anything but the most half-hearted
smile (however kindly) rather at Pound than at them. Their thick facetiousness
is of the rollicking slap-on-the-back order, suggesting another day and another
scene to ours. If they were better done and less conventional in their broad
unreality they would be welcome, like belated red-nosed comedians in the midst
of a series of turns too strictly designed to meet the ultra-feminine drawing-
room-entertainer taste, as a contrast. But they are not spirited enough to serve
even that purpose. They are a caricature of Pound attempting to deal with real
life—they are Pound at his worst.

If Pound had not a strain of absolutely authentic naïveté in him, had he
possessed the sort of minor sociable qualities that make the trivial adjustments

of the social world an open book to their possessor, he could not write in this clumsy and stupid way, when attempting to stage scenes from contemporary life. So though they represent Pound the artist at his worst, they show us, I believe, the true Pound, or that part that has not become incorporated in his best highly traditional poetry. And a simpleton is what we are left with. That natural and unvarnished, unassimilable, Pound, is the true child, which so many people in vain essay to be. But some inhibition has prevented him from getting that genuine naïf (which would have made him a poet) into his work. There, unfortunately, he always attitudinizes, frowns, struts, looks terribly knowing, 'breaks off,' shows off, puffs himself out, and so obscures the really simple, charming creature that he is.

From *Time and Western Man* (Boston: Beacon Press, 1957), pp. 72-74.

WILLIAM CARLOS WILLIAMS

Excerpts from a Critical Sketch:
A Draft of XXX Cantos by Ezra Pound

POUND HAS had the discernment to descry and the mind to grasp that the difficulties in which humanity finds itself need no phenomenal insight for their solution. Their cure is another matter, but that is no reason for a belief in a complicated mystery of approach fostered by those who wish nothing done, as it is no reason for a failure of the mind to function simply when dangerously confronted. Here is a theme: a closed mind which clings to its power—about which the intelligence beats seeking entrance. This is the basic theme of the *XXX Cantos.*

Reading them through consecutively, at one sitting (four hours) Pound's "faults" as a poet all center around his rancor against the malignant stupidity of a generation which polluted our rivers and would then, brightly, give ten or twenty or any imaginable number of millions of dollars as a fund toward the perpetuation of *Beauty*—in the form of a bequest to the New York Metropolitan Museum of Art.

"In America this crime has not been spread over a period of centuries, it has been done in the last twenty or twenty-five years, by the single generation, from fifteen to twenty-five years older than I am, who have held power through that slobbery period."

His versification has not as its objective (apparently) that of some contemporary verse of the best quality. It is patterned *still* after classic meters and so does often deform the natural order—though little and to a modified degree only (nor is his practice without advantages as a method). Pound does very definitely intend a modern speech—but wishes to save the excellences (well-worked-out forms) of the old, so leans to it overmuch.

A criticism of Pound's *Cantos* could not be better concerned, I think, than in considering them in relation to the principal move in imaginative writing today—that away from the word as a symbol toward the word as reality.

1) His words affect modernity with too much violence (at times)—a straining after slang effects, engendered by their effort to escape that which is their instinctive quality, a taking character from classic similes and modes. You cannot *easily* switch from Orteum to Peoria without violence (to the language). These images too greatly infest the *Cantos,* the words *cannot* escape being colored by them: 2) so too the form of the phrase—it affects a modern turn but is really bent to a classical beauty of image, so that in effect it often (though not always) mars the normal accent of speech. But not always: sometimes it is superbly done and Pound is always trying to overcome the difficulty.

Pound is humane in a like sense to that of the writer of the great cantos—without being in the least sentimental. He has been able to do this by paying attention first to his art, its difficulties, its opportunities: to language—as did Dante: to popular language—It is sheer stupidity to forget the primarily humane aspect of Dante's work in the rhapsodic swoon induced by his blinding technical, aesthetic and philosophic qualities.

All the thought and implications of thought are there in the words (in the minute character and relationships of the words—destroyed, avoided by . . .)—it is *that* I wish to say again and again—it is there in the technique and it is that that is the making or breaking of the work. It is that that one sees, feels. It is that that *is* the work of art—to be observed.

The means Pound has used for the realization of his effects—the poetry itself—:

It is beside the question to my mind to speak of Pound's versification as carefully and accurately measured—beyond all comparison——

Perhaps it is and if so, what of it?

That has nothing in it of value to recommend it. It is deeper than that. His excellence is that of the maker, not the measurer—I say he *is* a poet. This is in effect to have stepped beyond measure.

It is that the material is so molded that it is changed in *kind* from other statement. It is a *sort* beyond measure.

The measure is an inevitability, an unavoidable accessory after the fact. If one move, if one run, if one seize up a material—it cannot avoid having a measure, it cannot avoid a movement which clings to it—as the movement of a horse becomes a part of the rider also——

That is the way Pound's verse impresses me and why he can include pieces of prose and have them still part of a *poem*. It is incorporated in a movement of the intelligence which is special, beyond usual thought and action——

It partakes of a quality which makes the meter, the movement peculiar—unmeasurable (without a prior change of mind)——

It is that which is the evidence of invention. Pound's line is the movement of his thought, his concept of the whole——

As such, it has measure but not first to be picked at: certain realizable characteristics which may be looked at, evaluated more pointedly, then measured and "beautifully," "ideally," "correctly" pointed.

They (the lines) have a character that is parcel of the poem itself. (It is in the small make-up of the lines that the character of the poem definitely comes—and beyond which it cannot go.) . . .

How far has he succeeded? Generation, he says, as I interpret him, is analytical, it is not a mass fusion. Only superficially do the *Cantos* fuse the various temporal phases of the material Pound has chosen, into a synthesis. It is important to stress this for it is Pound's chief distinction in the *Cantos* —his personal point of departure from most that the modern is attempting. It is not by any means a synthesis, but a shot through all material—a true and somewhat old-fashioned analysis of his world.

It is still a Lenin striking through the mass, whipping it about, that engages his attention. That is the force Pound believes in. It is not a proletarian art—

He has succeeded against himself. He has had difficulties of training to overcome which he will not completely undo—in himself at least—if that were all.

But the words reveal it: white-gathered, sun-dazzle, rock-pool, god-sleight, sea-swirl, sea-break, vine-trunk, vine-must, pin-rack, glass-glint, wave-runs, salmon-pink, dew-haze, blue-shot, green-gold, green-ruddy, eye-glitter, blue-deep, wine-red, water-shift, rose-paleness, wave-cords, churn-stick.

We have, examining the work, successes—great ones—the first molds—clear cut, never turgid, not following the heated trivial—staying cold, "classical" but swift with a movement of thought.

It stands out from almost all other verse by a faceted quality that is not muzzy, painty, wet. It is a dry, clean use of words. Yet look at the words. They are themselves not dead. They have not been violated by "thinking." They have been used willingly by thought.

Imagistic use has entirely passed out of them, there is almost no use of simile, no allegory—the word has been used in its plain sense to represent a thing—remaining thus loose in its context—not gummy—(when at its best)—an objective unit in the design—but alive.

Pound has taken them up—if it may be risked—alertly, swiftly, but with feeling for the delicate living quality in them—not disinfecting, scraping them, but careful of the life. The result is that they stay living—and discreet. . . .

From *Selected Essays of William Carlos Williams* (New York: New Directions, 1931), pp. 106-108, 110-11.

ALLEN TATE

On Ezra Pound's *Cantos*

THE SECRET of his form is this: conversation. The *Cantos* are talk, talk, talk; not by anyone in particular to anyone else in particular; they are just rambling talk. At least each canto is a cunningly devised imitation of a casual conversation in which no one presses any subject very far. The length of breath, the span of conversational energy, is the length of a canto. The conversationalist pauses; there is just enough unfinished business left hanging in the air to give him a new start; so that the transitions between the cantos are natural and easy.

Each canto has the broken flow and the somewhat elusive climax of a good monologue: because there is no single speaker, it is a many-voiced monologue. That is the method of the poems—though there is another quality of the form that I must postpone for a moment—*and that is what the poems are about.*

There are, as I have said, three subjects of conversation—ancient times, Renaissance Italy, and the present—but these are not what the *Cantos* are about. They are not about Italy, nor about Greece, nor are they about us. They are not about anything. But they are distinguished verse. Mr. Pound himself tells us:

> And they want to know what we talked about? *"de litteris et*
> *de armis, praestantibus ingeniis,*
> Both of ancient times and our own; books, arms,
> And men of unusual genius
> Both of ancient times and our own, in short the usual subjects
> Of conversation between intelligent men."

. . . Mr. Pound is a typically modern, rootless, and internationalized intelligence. In the place of the traditional supernaturalism of the older and local cultures, he has a cosmopolitan curiosity that seeks out marvels, which are all equally marvelous, whether it be a Greek myth or the antics in Europe of a lady from Kansas. He has the bright, cosmopolitan *savoir faire* which refuses to be "taken in": he will not believe, being a traditionalist at bottom, that the "perverts, who have set money-lust before the pleasures of the senses," are better than swine. And ironically, being modern and a hater of modernity, he sees all history as deformed by the trim-coifed goddess.

The *Cantos* are a book of marvels—marvels that he has read about, or heard of, or seen; there are Greek myths, tales of Italian feuds, meetings with strange people, rumors of intrigues of state, memories of remarkable dead friends like

T. E. Hulme, comments on philosophical problems, harangues on abuses of the age; the "usual subjects of conversation between intelligent men."

It is all fragmentary. Now nearly every canto begins with a bit of heroic antiquity, some myth, or classical quotation, or a lovely piece of lyrical description in a grand style. It invariably breaks down. It trails off into a piece of contemporary satire, or a flat narrative of the rascality of some Italian prince. This is the special quality of Mr. Pound's form, the essence of his talk, the direction of these magnificent conversations.

For not once does Mr. Pound give himself up to any single story or myth. The thin symbolism from the Circe myth is hardly more than a leading tone, an unconscious prejudice about men which he is not willing to indicate beyond the barest outline. He cannot believe in myths, much less in his own power of imagining them out to a conclusion. None of his myths is compelling enough to draw out his total intellectual resources; none goes far enough to become a belief or even a momentary fiction. They remain marvels to be looked at, but they are meaningless, the wrecks of civilization. His powerful juxtapositions of the ancient, the Renaissance, and the modern worlds reduce all three elements to an unhistorical miscellany, timeless and without origin, and no longer a force in the lives of men.

From *Essays of Four Decades* (Chicago: The Swallow Press, 1968), pp. 364-71.

R. P. BLACKMUR

An Adjunct to the Muses' Diadem

"IN THE gloom, the gold gathers the light against it." It does not matter much what source the gloom has in folly and misjudgment and human dark, if within the gloom the gold still gathers the light against it. The line occurs in Pound's eleventh Canto, one of those dealing with Sigismondo Malatesta, written about 1922, and thus, I think, at the heart of that period of Pound's work which shows most light because there was most gold to gather it, the period between 1918 and 1928: the period of Propertius in Pound's remaking, of the translations from the Provençal, of *Hugh Selwyn Mauberley,* and of the first *Thirty Cantos.* Let us see, knowing the dimness is only of time, what is (in Marianne Moore's phrase) "not now more magnificent than it is dim."

Take the line itself once more—"In the gloom, the gold gathers the light against it"; does it not commit itself in the memory by coming at an absolute image, good anywhere the writs of language run, by the most ordinary possible means, the fused sequences of two trains of alliteration, the one guttural and the other dental? Does it not also, and more important, clinch the alliteration and the image by displaying itself, as Pound used to argue all verse ought to display itself, in the sequence, not of the metronome, but of the musical phrase? Do we not come, thus, on a true blank verse line where something, which we here call music, lasts when the words have stopped, and which locks, or gears, the words together when they are spoken? Nobody knows whether the words discover the music or the music discovers the unity in the words; nobody but a craftsman skilled at this particular job of work knows how to make words and music work in common with so little contextual or environmental force; without a drama or a situation; nobody, that is, but a craftsman skilled in the details of other men's work. "In the gloom, the gold gathers the light against it."

In the eighth Canto, there is a running version of Malatesta's own lines beginning *O Spreti che gia fusti in questy regny,* which reads as follows:

> Ye spirits who of olde were in this land
> Each under Love, and shaken,
> Go with your lutes, awaken
> The summer within her mind,
> Who hath not Helen for peer
> > Yseut nor Batsabe.

Here again it is composition.in the sequence of the musical phrase which lifts
this most commonplace and traditional notion to the direct freshness of music,
and without, as in songs actually sung, any disfigurement or blurring of the
words. We resume, by the skill of the words and their order, not only the
tradition but also the feeling that gave rise to the tradition, but we in no way
repeat the localized version of the tradition that Malatesta himself used in (what
would be) bad English of the twentieth century pretending to be fifteenth.
Another example, the "Alba" from *Langue d'Oc,* carries this variety of composition about as far as Pound, as craftsman, could force it. It is again translation.

> When the nightingale to his mate
> Sings day-long and night late
> My love and I keep state
>   In bower,
>   In flower,
>   Till the watchman on the tower
> Cry:
>   "Up! Thou rascal, Rise,
>   I see the white
>   Light
>   And the night
>   Flies."

Here, it is true, we are nearer both the regular or metronomic pattern and an
actual singing tune, but we are there by exactly the means of musical composition; we have only to think how Swinburne would have done it, to see
the delicacy and absoluteness of Pound's musical phrase, and the difference is
to be named by thinking of what Pound called, and here made present, the
"prose tradition in verse." That tradition, that verse ought to be at least as well
written as prose, is exemplified, when one has caught its idiosyncrasy of
movement, in passage after passage of the *Homage to Sextus Propertius,* nowhere
better for purposes of quotation than the opening of the sixth selection.

> When, when, and whenever death closes our eyelids,
> Moving naked over Acheron
>   Upon the one raft, victor and conquered together,
> Marius and Jugurtha together,
>   one tangle of shadows.

The third and fourth lines in this passage are not at all the same thing as what
Propertius wrote, nor do they need to have been for what Pound was doing.

> Victor cum victis pariter miscebitur umbris:
> consule cum Mario, capte Iugurtha, sedes

is magnificent formal Latin with the special kind of finality that goes with that mode of language and that kind of musical creation in language. Pound used what he could catch of the mood in Propertius' mind—not the mode of his language—and responded to it with what he could make out of the best current mood and mode of his own time; that is why his versions of Propertius are called a Homage, and that is why they seem written in a mode of language (the prose tradition combined with composition in the musical phrase) which is an addition to the language itself. One more passage should suggest the characteristics of that mode.

> But for something to read in normal circumstances?
> For a few pages brought down from the forked hill unsullied?
> I ask a wreath which will not crush my head.
>   And there is no hurry about it;
> I shall have, doubtless, a boom after my funeral,
> Seeing that long standing increases all things
>   regardless of quality.

This and the "Alba" quoted above are the extremes in opposite directions to which Pound brought his special mode; his very best work, the extreme of his own accomplishment, comes about when his mode is running in both directions at once, sometimes in the *Cantos,* sometimes in the two groups of poems called *Hugh Selwyn Mauberley,* and it is from these groups that we may select four examples. One is the fifth and concluding passage from the "Ode pour l'Election de son Sépulchre."

> There died a myriad,
> And of the best among them,
> For an old bitch gone in the teeth,
> For a botched civilization,
>
> Charm, smiling at the good mouth,
> Quick eyes gone under earth's lid,
>
> For two gross of broken statues,
> For a few thousand battered books.

"In the gloom, the gold gathers the light against it." There is no better poem of the other war, and it may well come to be that there is no better poem to herald the war just over, when we see what has happened in it. One feels like addressing Pound as Williams addressed the morning star: "Shine alone in the sunrise, towards which you lend no part." The central distich, once the context, both that before and the concluding distich, has been mastered, makes both epitaph and epigraph, both as near breathless and as near sound as words can be. It is Propertius *and* the poets of the Langue d'Oc that wrote them, the

sequence of the musical phrase *and* the prose tradition in verse, but leaning
a little more strongly toward Propertius and prose than Arnaut and music.

A little nearer to Arnaut, but not much, is a quatrain from the preceding
section of the same ode, but only by reason of the rhymes. It needs no context:

> Faun's flesh is not to us,
> Nor the saint's vision.
> We have the press for wafer;
> Franchise for circumcision.

It is prose in syntax; generalized or commonplace in thought; but it is prose
and commonplace moving into music through a combination of its alliterative
sequence—its ear for syllabic relations and their development—and the sequence of the idiomatic phrase. We can see—or hear—this more clearly if we
put it next to two quatrains from "Medallion," where the syllabic play is as
complex in English as Arnaut or Bertrans in Provençal, and where the rhyming
is Pound's own.

> Luini in porcelain!
> The grand piano
> Utters a profane
> Protest with her clear soprano.
>
> The sleek head emerges
> From the gold-yellow frock
> As Anadyomene in the opening
> Pages of Reinach.

Eliot says that we must not be deceived by the roughness of the rhyme in these
poems, but I do not see how anybody could see anything rough about a metric
and syllabic practice which keep, as these lines do, all their sounds in the ear
at once without blur or whir or anything but their own clear creation, as in
this:

> Go, dumb-born book,
> Tell her that sang me once that song of Lawes;
> Hadst thou but song
> As thou has subjects known,
> Then were there cause in thee that should condone
> Even my faults that heavy upon me lie
> And build her glories their longevity.
> Tell her that sheds
>
> Such treasure in the air,
> Recking naught else but that her graces give
> Life to the moment,
> I would bid them live
> As roses might, in magic amber laid,

> Red overwrought with orange and all made
> One substance and one color
> Braving time.

These are the first two stanzas of the "Envoi (1919)" to the first part of *Hugh Selwyn Mauberley,* and they are quoted last in our series of examples because, at least in the context here provided for them, they show almost perfectly the combination wanted—of the prose tradition and the musical phrase; and because, too, with some alteration of the pronouns, they are lines that might well be addressed to Pound himself—except on those occasions when he gave up his song (the subjects he had mastered as music) for the sake of subjects so-called (songs which he had not mastered); for when he tried such subjects his poems are left so many

> Mouths biting empty air,
> The still stone dogs,
> Caught in metamorphosis, were
> Left him as epilogues;

just as when he kept to the songs he knew, he produced "Ultimate affronts to human redundancies"—than which a poet of Pound's class can do nothing more.

But what is Pound's class, and how can it be described without any contemptuousness in the description and without giving the effect of anything contemptible in the class; for it is an admirable class and ought to be spoken of with admiration. Essentially it is the class of those who have a care for the purity of the tongue as it is spoken and as it sounds and as it changes in speech and sound, and who know that that purity can only exist in the movement of continuous alternation between the "faun's flesh and the saint's vision," and who know, so, that the movement, not the alternatives themselves, is the movement of music.

It is the purity of language conceived as the mind's agency for creation or discovery, not merely manipulation or communication, that this class of poet works for; it is, so to speak, a pitch or condition of speech almost without reference to its particular content in a given work. The class is common enough, short of the work; it is the class of those everywhere who talk and read for the sake of talking and reading, the class of spontaneous appreciators; but it is a very uncommon class at the level of active work, and it is the active workers who make appreciation possible by providing immediate examples to train taste. It is executive work; it shows what can be done with the instrument by skill and continuous practice, and it reminds us, in terms of new prospects, of what has been done. But even more than those who read, those who write need the continuous example of poets supreme in the executive class or they would not know either what they ought to do or what it is possible for them to do in the collaboration between their conceptions and their language. Poets like Pound are the executive artists for their generation; he does not provide a new way of looking, and I think Eliot is mistaken in thinking his work an example

of Arnold's criticism of life, but he provides the *means* of many ways of looking.
If you criticize Pound for what he has said you come on the ancient commonplace refreshed through conventions that are immediately available; without
his craftsmanship he would be a "popular" poet in the pejorative sense: the
convention is always interposed *between* the actuality and his reaction to it; even
his best verse is only applicable to *other* situations, it never creates its own. But
that is precisely what makes him so valuable to other poets, both good and
bad; his executive example helps them to unite reaction and actuality directly
in a convention—the necessary working together—of language and conception,
not now a commonplace but a commonplace to come; and his work affords
that help because it does not intrude any conception or contortion of conception
of its own. Thus he differs from poets like Hopkins or Rimbaud or Swinburne
or Whitman, whose innovations represented sometimes weaknesses and sometimes purposes of their own, which when imitated substitute for weaknesses
in their imitators. Thus also, he differs from poets like Shakespeare or Dante
or Wordsworth, from whom the modern poet learns less the means of his trade
than he learns habits of feeling to transpose and habits of insights to translate
and habits of architecture—of large composition—of which he will probably
be incapable except in intent. He is like, rather, poets like Cavalcanti, Arnaut,
Gautier (his own chosen example), Marlowe, Greene, and Herrick; all of whom
strike the living writer as immediately useful in his trade, but in no way
affecting the life he puts into his trade.

In short, poets of the class in which Pound shines are of an absolute
preliminary necessity for the continuing life of poetry. What he meant by
composition in the sequence of the musical phrase and by the prose tradition
in verse, both as he taught them in his criticism and as he exhibited them in
his translations and original verses, were not only necessary in 1912 or 1918,
but are necessary now and have always been necessary if the work done by
man's mind in verse is not to fall off and forget its possibilities. "In the gloom,
the gold gathers the light against it." If the first word in the last line is taken
in the opposite sense, as in his easy irony he meant it to be taken, we can apply
to Pound once more in our own context, the following verses which he once
applied to himself:

> His true Penelope was Flaubert,
> He fished by obstinate isles;
> Observed the elegance of Circe's hair
> Rather than the mottoes on sun-dials.
>
> Unaffected by "the march of events,"
> He passed from men's memory in *l'an trentiesme*
> *De son eage,* the case presents
> No adjunct to the Muses' diadem.

From *Form and Value in Modern Poetry* (New York: Anchor Books, 1957),
pp. 113-20.

YVOR WINTERS

Ezra Pound's Techniques

THE TERM *qualitative progression* I am borrowing from Mr. Kenneth Burke's volume of criticism, *Counterstatement,* to which I have already had several occasions to refer. This method arises from the same attitudes as the last, and it resembles the last except that it makes no attempt whatever at a rational progression. Mr. Pound's *Cantos*[1] are the perfect example of the form; they make no unfulfilled claims to matter not in the poetry, or at any rate relatively few and slight claims. Mr. Pound proceeds from image to image wholly through the coherence of feeling: his sole principle of unity is mood, carefully established and varied. That is, each statement he makes is reasonable in itself, but the progression from statement to statement is not reasonable: it is the progression either of random conversation or of revery. This kind of progression might be based upon an implicit rationality; in such a case the rationality of the progression becomes clearly evident before the poem has gone very far and is never thereafter lost sight of; in a poem of any length such implicit rationality would have to be supported by explicit exposition. But in Mr. Pound's poem I can find few implicit themes of any great clarity, and fewer still that are explicit.[2]

The principle of selection being less definite, the selection of details is presumably less rigid, though many of the details display a fine quality. The symbolic range is therefore reduced, since the form reduces the importance of

1. *A Draft of XXX Cantos,* by Ezra Pound. Hours Press: 15 rue Guénégaud: Paris: 1930.
2. Mr. Pound, writing in The New English Weekly, Vol. III, No. 4, of remarks similar to the above which I published in The Hound and Horn for the Spring of 1933, states: "I am convinced that one should not as a general rule reply to critics or defend works in process of being written. On the other hand, if one prints fragments of a work one perhaps owes the benevolent reader enough explanation to prevent his wasting time in unnecessary misunderstanding.

"The nadir of solemn and elaborate imbecility is reached by Mr. Winters in an American publication where he deplores my 'abandonment of logic in the Cantos,' presumably because he has never read my prose criticism and has never heard of the ideographic method, and thinks logic is limited to a few 'forms of logic' which better minds were already finding inadequate to the mental needs of the XIIIth century."

As to the particular defects of scholarship which Mr. Pound attributes to me, he is, alas, mistaken. For the rest, one may only say that civilization rests on the recognition that language possesses both connotative and denotative powers; that the abandonment of one in a poem impoverishes the poem to that extent; and that the abandonment of the denotative, or rational, in particular, and in a pure state, results in one's losing the only means available for checking up on the qualitative or "ideographic" sequences to see if they really are coherent in more than vague feeling. Mr. Pound, in other words, has no way of knowing whether he can think or not.

selectiveness, or self-directed action. The movement is proportionately slow and
wavering—indeed is frequently shuffling and undistinguished—and the range
of material handled is limited: I do not mean that the poetry cannot refer to
a great many types of actions and persons, but that it can find in them little
variety of value—it refers to them all in the same way, that is, casually. Mr.
Pound resembles a village loafer who sees much and understands little.

The following passage, however, the opening of the fourth *Canto,* illustrates
this kind of poetry at its best:

> Palace in smoky light,
> Troy but a heap of smouldering boundary stones,
> ANAXIFORMINGES! *Aurunculeia!*
> Hear me, Cadmus of Golden Prows!
> The silver mirrors catch the bright stones and flare,
> Dawn, to our waking, drifts in the cool green light;
> Dew-haze blurs, in the grass, pale ankles moving.
> Beat, beat, whirr, thud, in the soft turf under the apple-trees,
> Choros nympharum, goat-foot, with the pale foot alternate;
> Crescent of blue-shot waters, green-gold in the shallows,
> A black cock crows in the sea-foam;

The loveliness of such poetry appears to me indubitable, but it is merely a blur
of revery: its tenuity becomes apparent if one compares it, for example, to the
poetry of Paul Valéry, which achieves effects of imagery, particularly of at-
mospheric imagery, quite as extraordinary, along with precision, depth of
meaning, and the power that comes of close and inalterable organization, and,
though Mr. Pound's admirers have given him a great name as a metrist, with
incomparably finer effects of sound. . . .

The poet who has made the most ambitious attempt of our century to create
a carry-all form is Ezra Pound, but his free verse, though the best of it is better
meter than any of the neo-Websterian verse, remains in spite of his efforts a
lyrical instrument which is improperly used for other than lyrical effects.

As in all free verse, and as in Websterian verse, we have in Mr. Pound's
verse no normal foot, nothing to take the place of the couplet's basic regularity,
no substructure insisting steadily on the identity of the poem, regardless of
whither it wander. The meter, as in nearly all free verse, is wholly at one with
the mood, and if the mood undergoes a marked change, the whole poem goes
off with it and becomes incoherent. Purely didactic poetry is impossible in the
form, because of the chanting, emotional quality of the rhythms, from which
there is no escape, even momentarily: the rhythm implies a limited lyrical
mood.

Unlike the Websterians, Mr. Pound in his best *Cantos* does not muddy his
verse with secondary and uncontrolled didacticism: he is usually didactic, if at
all, by implication only, but implication is inadequate, in the long run, as a
didactic instrument. In the best *Cantos,* [3] at least, Mr. Pound is successful,

3. *A Draft of Thirty Cantos,* by Ezra Pound. Hours Press: Paris: 1932.

whether in fragments or on the whole, but he presents merely a psychological progression or flux, the convention being sometimes that of wandering revery, sometimes that of wandering conversation. The range of such a convention is narrowly limited, not only as regards formulable content, but as regards feeling. The feelings attendant upon revery and amiable conversation tend to great similarity notwithstanding the subject matter, and they simply are not the most vigorous or important feelings of which the human being is capable.

The method, when employed in satirical portraiture, lacks the incisiveness of the eighteenth century masters:

> So we lëft him at läst in Chiässo
> Alöng with the old wöman from Känsas,
> Sólid Känsas, her däughter had märried that Swïss
> Who këpt the Buffët in Chiässo.
> Did it shäke her? It dïd not shäke her.
> She sät thére in the wäiting róom, sólid Känsas,
> Stïff as a cigär store Ïndian from the Böwery
> Süch as óne säw in the nïneties,
> First söd of blëeding Känsas
> That had prodüced this lïgneous sölidness.
> If thóu wilt gö to Chiässo wilt find that indestrüctible fëmale
> As if wäiting for the träin to Topëka.

The passage is amusing in a way, but is soft and diffuse. Even *The Rosciad* affords more successful portraits. Notwithstanding the concreteness of the material, the meter is already outside the range in which it functions most effectively—the range, that is, of the fourth or of the seventh Canto. The meter is naturally elegiac, and the handling of it in such a passage as this is bound to be arbitrary and insensitive: the secondary accents fall accidentally, are hard to identify, and are neither perceptive nor intrinsically pleasing as sound, and so little attention is paid to shadings of quantity as to render the passage very awkward of movement. These defects in general are the defects of Mr. Pound's style, though in many passages they are far less evident than here. Like Swinburne, he has acquired an undeserved reputation for metrical mastery, largely as a result of a fairly suave manipulation of certain insistently recurring mannerisms, which, to the half-trained or the half-alert, appear signs of finish and control rather than what they are, the signs of a measure of incertitude and of insensitivity.

Mr. Pound has come no closer than Mr. Tate to creating a carry-all meter, but in his efforts he has sometimes created a purer poetry than has Mr. Tate while indulging in strictly similar efforts, chiefly, perhaps, because Mr. Pound has not been aware of comparably difficult material.

From *In Defense of Reason* (Chicago: The Swallow Press, 1947), pp. 57-59, 145-46.

RICHARD EBERHART

An Approach to the *Cantos*

THINGS AS they were or are. Things as they are said or thought to be. Things as they ought to be. Aristotle, lastly here, says a poet must of necessity imitate one of these three objects. Pound's history eschews the first. He cannot encompass the third, due perhaps to the secular nature of the intentions of the work. His tirades against banks, money, political machinators, would come under this category, but announce artistic limitations. There is no entire moral or ethical view of man in the sense that Pound is presenting the world as it ought to be. He harangues against usury, but offers no complete economic platform, only negative criticism. There is no espousal of a Ghandian agrarianism, or of a world state, or any solution theoretically posed. Indeed, it seems a rebuke and limitation that Pound, so roundly smashing idols as he thinks with negative criticism, has not been inventive enough to propose an imaginative solution to the dilemma of man. But where is there one, from a secular departure? He is much too intelligent to think that there is any. But he is not as wise as the makers of scripture. And the Cantos can be richly enjoyed as poetry.

Things as they are thought to be. Pound is the maker of his own conception of events as he thinks them to be. His conception embraces entire histories East and West, the rise and fall of civilizations, the reappearance in one country of political intrigues known in another in a different century, the evil in man cropping up everywhere, the aristocracy of art also recurrent ("to sort out the animals" 80), Chororua equated with Taishan, "The enormous tragedy of the dream in the peasant's bent shoulders" (74), but "Fear god and the stupidity of the populace" (74); "Entered the Bros Watson's store in Clinton, N. Y." (77) related to "The cakeshops of the Nevsky" (78), et sic de similibus.

Pound has a handle on the truth and carries history along with him in his case, wearing a gaudy suit of motley. As history, the Cantos are not impressive; as reconstructed history they are a vessel of wonder: as poetry, they are in their element. History, linguistics, economics, sociology, myth are all brought together documentarily, in the weaving of a rich tapestry. I think of the Cantos as a mosaic, or a tapestry, as of an intricate ancient work put together with incredible skill and patience over a long period of time, a Uccello in colored silks.

The new Cantos (74-84) are in some ways more nervous, elliptical, incoherent, lyrical than their predecessors. The lyrical quality is a boon, and the wiry liveliness is highly stimulating. One might make out a point that his later work in some way approaches surrealism, although it does not arrive there. This is odd in view of the hard, prosaic actuality of much of the past writing. Someone might study the more effusive, lyrical quality discoverable in the present Cantos in comparison with the more nearly incipient lyricism in the earlier. Also cogent would be a study of the Cantos in relation to musical structure; the present Cantos abound in melody, in melodic refrain. The subtlety of the spacing of the repetitions of phrase, and their metamorphoses, are cunningly contrived in an orchestration of sound and sense.

The art of teaching is to suggest. Pound is in one facet the frustrated teacher neurotically forced because his pupils do not know about, or enough about, or qualitatively enough about Padre Jose Elizonida, Kung, taou, Chung, Kung futsen, Tangwan Kung, or Tsze Sze's third thesis. He wants them to know about these. He lays them out to view in a long fury of explication. He ends by stuffing them down the throats of his readers. After the *nth* reference to *x,* how many of his readers will be provoked to refer to, study, and inwardly digest that individual or datum? The error is that of explication, and of explication, of incomplete explication. And of explication, perversely that it is not evocation. Pound is all on the outside of the mind. The work is all brains, no soul. Or better, not sufficiently humane in brain, not deep enough in soul. We do not go to the Cantos for knowledge. We go to them with our own knowledge for revisions of feeling, for accretions of new feelings.

From "Pound's New Cantos," *Quarterly Review of Literature,* 5 (1949), 174-91.

RAY B. WEST

Ezra Pound and Contemporary Criticism

ELIOT ONCE wrote that the first half of the twentieth century would eventually become known as "The Age of Ezra Pound." This is undoubtedly an exaggeration of fact, but as a metaphor it will do. Pound lead in the reintroduction of Dante to the present age and in the recognition of the late nineteenth century *symboliste* poets. He introduced the concept of literary history as a continuing or ever-recurring present, thus not only piercing the walls of pragmatic scholarship, but reviving the works of Homer, Catullus, Propertius, Ovid, Dante, and the Provencal poets.

> It is dawn at Jerusalem while midnight hovers above the pillars of Hercules. All ages are contemporaneous. It is b.c., let us say, in Morocco. The Middle Ages are in Russia [1910]. The future stirs already in the minds of the few. This is especially true of literature, where the real time is independent of the apparent, and where many dead men are our grandchildren's contemporaries, while many of our contemporaries have already been gathered into Abraham's bosom.

Except for Pound's unique style, such a statement might have come from Eliot's "Tradition and the Individual Talent," and it and other comparable statements undoubtedly had a great deal to do with Eliot's views.

Pound pioneered in the revival of Stendhal and James, and in the recognition of such contemporary authors as James Joyce, D. H. Lawrence, and Eliot. Through his early interest in imagism, his later preoccupation with the Chinese character studies of Ernest Fenollosa, and his feeling "that poetry ought to be as well written as prose," he undoubtedly had a great deal to do with the trend away from the lyrical and sentimental traditions in English in American verse. During his period with Eliot in London, he wrote,

> that at a particular date in a particular room, two authors . . . decided that the dilutation of *vers libre,* Amygism, Lee Masterism, general floppiness had gone too far and that some counter-current must be set doing. . . . Results: Poems in Mr. Eliot's *second* volume, not contained in his first ['Prufrock', *Egoist,* 1917], also 'H. S. Mauberly.'

Perhaps his greatest contribution, however, and one which has exercised the most complete shift of emphasis in twentieth century criticism and in the teaching of literature, was his insistence that scholars and critics focus their attention upon the works themselves. "My opinion of critics," he once wrote,

> is that: the best are those who actually cause an amelioration in the art which they criticize. The next best are those who most focus attention on the best that is written (or painted or composed or cut in stone). And the pestilential vermin are those who detract attention *from* the best, either to the second rate, or to hokum, or to their own critical writing.

Pound believed that "All teaching of literature should be performed by the presentation and juxtaposition of specimens of writing and NOT by discussion of some other discusser's opinion *about* the general standing of a poet or author." His own method in his examination of James's novels was, briefly, as follows: first, a brief review of the principal characters and the action; second, a quotation from sections of the work; third, interpretations, a critical raising of questions, and an estimation of the value of method and content. . . .

Pound's career has steadily aimed at what has popularly become known as "a correction of taste," and there is justification for the raising of Dante to the level which Shakespeare occupied during the nineteenth century, if for no other reason than to suggest to the ordinary student the possibility of values outside the English tongue. There is a like justification for introducing to American teachers of literature an awareness of world literature, for as Pound wrote in *Polite Essays:* "Homer, Villon, Propertius, speak of the world as I know it, whereas Mr. Tennyson and Dr. Bridges did not," and several generations of American schoolboys (including Pound's own generation) had focussed upon Tennyson at the expense of literature exceedingly more pertinent and valuable to them.

It seems finally that Pound's reputation as a critic will rest upon those measures of "correction" which he introduced, rather than upon any total or systematic view of literature. Artists he considered "the antenna of the race," the "registering instruments; and if they falsify their reports there is no measures to the harm that they do." To critics and teachers, he said, the teaching or evaluation of literature in general terms or in terms not directly relating to the work of art itself is "inexcusable AFTER the era of 'Agassiz and the fish'—by which I mean now that general education is in a position to profit by the parallels of biological study based on EXAMINATION and COMPARISON of particular specimens." These two points, considering the influence they have had upon our concept of the creative process, the critical act, and upon the educational theories of this age, are quite enough to assure him a position of eminence in the history of criticism in the twentieth century.

From "Ezra Pound and Contemporary Criticism," *Quarterly Review of Literature,* 5 (1949), 192-200.

JOHN BERRYMAN

The Poetry of Ezra Pound

WHY HAS Pound translated so much? The question is an important one, and the answers usually given ignore the abyss of difference between his just-translations, like the Cavalcanti (the Canzone aside, of which his final version opens Canto XXXVI), such as might have been made by another poet of superlative skill, and renderings like those in *Cathay* and *Propertius,* which are part of Pound's own life-poetry. The first class may be considered as exercise, propaganda, critical activity, taken in conjunction with his incoherent and powerful literary criticism. The second class requires a word about Pound's notion of *personae* or masks, which issued successively in the masks of Cino, Bertran de Born, various Chinese poets, Propertius, Mauberley, fifty others. They differ both from Yeats's masks and from the dramatizations, such as Prufrock and Auden's 'airman,' that other poets find necessary in a period inimical to poetry, gregarious, and impatient of dignity.

We hear of the notion in two of his earliest poems, a sonnet 'Masks' about

> souls that found themselves among
> Unwonted folk that spake a hostile tongue,
> Some souls from all the rest who'd not forgot
> The star-span acres of a former lot
> Where boundless mid the clouds his course he swung,
> Or carnate with his elder brothers sung
> E'er ballad makers lisped of Camelot. . . .

and 'In Durance':

> But for all that, I am homesick after mine own kind
> And would meet kindred even as I am,
> Flesh-shrouded bearing the secret.

The question is, what the masks are *for?*

Does any reader who is familiar with Pound's poetry really not see that its subject is life of the modern poet? . . . It is in 'N. Y.' of *Rispostes* (1912), the volume in which Pound established his manner and the volume with which modern poetry in English may be felt to have begun—

> My City, my beloved, my white! Ah, slender,

. . . . .

Delicately upon the reed, attend me!

Now do I know that I am mad,
For here are a million people surly with traffic:
This is no maid.
Neither could I play upon any reed if I had one.

It is everywhere (as well as in the Chinese work) in the more 'original' poems
and epigrams of *Lustra*, written 1913-1916. (A lustrum is 'an offering for the
sins of the whole people, made by the censors at the expiration of their five
years of office.' It has not perhaps been sufficiently observed that Pound is one
of the wittiest poets who ever wrote. Yet he is serious enough in this title.
In certain attitudes—his medieval nostalgia, literary anti-semitism, others—he
a good deal resembles Henry Adams; each spent his life, as it were, seeking
an official post where he could be used, and their failure to find one produced
both the freedom and the inconsequence that charm and annoy us in these
authors.) It is in the elaborate foreign personae that followed, *Cathay* (1915)—

> And I have moped in the Emperor's garden, awaiting
> an order-to-write!

and *Propertius* (1917)—

> I who come first from the clear font
> Bringing the Grecian orgies into Italy
>   and the dance into Italy.

It is in *Mauberly*, of course—

> Dowson found harlots cheaper than hotels;
> So spoke the author of "The Dorian Mood,"

> M. Verog, out of step with the decade,
> Detached from his contemporaries,
> Neglected by the young,
> Because of these reveries.

Meanwhile Pound's concept of method had been strongly affected by Ernest
Fenollosa's essay on *The Chinese Written Character as a Medium for Poetry*
('Metaphor, the revealer of nature, is the very substance of poetry. . . . Chinese
poetry gets back near to the processes of nature by means of its vivid figure. . . .
If we attempt to follow it in English we must use words highly charged, words
whose vital suggestion shall interplay as nature interplays. Sentences must be
like the mingling of the fringes of feathered banners, or as the colors of many
flowers blended into the single sheen of a meadow. . . . a thousand tints of

verb') and for years he had been trying to work out a form whereby he could get his subject all together; by the time of *Mauberley* he had succeeded, in the final version of the opening *Cantos*. And it is, as we shall see, in the *Cantos* also.

Above all, certain themes in the life of the modern poet: indecision-decision and infidelity-fidelity. Pound has written much more love-poetry than is generally realized, and when fidelity and decision lock in his imagination we hear extraordinary effects, passionate, solemn. A lady is served her singer-lover's hearts, eats, and her husband tells her whose:

> "It is Cabestan's heart in the dish."
> "It is Cabestan's heart in the dish?
> "No other taste shall change this."   (Canto IV)

She hurtles from the window.

> And in south province Tchin Tiaouen had risen
> and took the city of Tchang tcheou
> offered marriage to Ouang Chi,
> who said: It is an honour.
> I must first bury Kanouen. His body is heavy.
> His ashes were light to carry
> Bright was the flame for Kanouen
>   Ouang Chi cast herself into it, Faithful forever
>   High the hall TIMOUR made her.   (Canto LVI)

'His body is heavy.' The theme produces also the dazzle and terror of the end of 'Near Perigord,' where we finally reach Bertran *through Maent*, whom we'd despaired of. If there are a passion and solemnity beyond this in poetry—

> Soul awful! if the earth has ever lodg'd
> An awful soul—

we have to go far to find them. If Pound is neither the poet apostrophized here nor the poet apostrophizing, not Milton or Wordsworth, his place will be high enough. These themes of decision and fidelity bear on much besides love in his poetry, and even—as one would expect with a subject of the poet-in-exile (Ovid, Dante, Villon, Browning, Henry James, Joyce, Pound, Eliot, as Mann, Brecht, Auden) whose allegiance is to an ideal state—upon politics:

> homage, fealty are to the person
>   can not be to body politic. . . .   (Canto LXVII)[1]

1. Without allusion to the poet's personal situation, which is rather a matter for courts, which have reached no verdict, and psychiatrists, who have declared the poet insane, than for literary criticism, it will be recalled as a gloss for these lines that when the Irish patriot Sir Roger Casement was tried for treason a war ago he had to be tried under a statute centuries old, the charge being

Of course there are other themes, strong and weak, and a multiplicity of topics, analogies to the life of the modern poet, with or without metaphor the *interests* of the poet. But this would appear to characterize any poet's work. I mean more definitely 'Life and Contacts,' as the sub-title of *Hugh Selwyn Mauberley* has it.

It is not quite Ezra Pound himself. Yeats, another Romantic, was also the subject of his own poetry, himself-as-himself. Pound is his own subject *qua* modern poet; it is the experience and fate of this writer 'born / In a half savage country, out of date,' a voluntary exile for over thirty years, that concern him. Another distinction is necessary. Wallace Stevens has presented us in recent years with a series of strange prose documents about 'imagination' and 'reality.' If Mr. Stevens' poetry has for substance imagination, in this dichotomy, Pound's has for substance reality. A poem like 'Villanelle: the Psychological Hour' or the passage I have quoted about Swinburne could have been made only by Pound, and the habit of mind involved has given us much truth that we could not otherwise have had. Two young friends did not come to see the poet! The poet missed a master! This is really in part what life consists of, though reading most poetry one would never guess it.

> And we say good-bye to you also,
> For you seem never to have discovered
> That your relationship is wholly parasitic;
> Yet to our feasts you bring neither
> Wit, nor good spirits, nor the pleasing attitudes
> Of discipleship.

It is personal, but it is not very personal. The 'distance' everywhere felt in the finest verse that treats his subject directly has I think two powerful sources, apart from the usual ones (versification and so on). First, there is the peculiar detachment of interest with which Pound seems to regard himself; no writer could be less revelatory of his passional life, and his friends have recorded—Dr. Williams with annoyance—the same life-long reticence in private. Second, his unfaltering, encyclopedic mastery of tone—a mastery that compensates for a comparative weakness of syntax. (By instinct, I parenthesize, Pound has always minimized the importance of syntax, and this instinct perhaps accounts for his inveterate dislike for Milton, a dislike that has had broad consequences for three decades of the twentieth century; not only did Milton seem to him, perhaps, anti-romantic *and* anti-realistic, undetailed, and anti-conversational, but Milton is the supreme English master of syntax.) Behind this mastery lies his ear. I scarcely know what to say of Pound's ear. Fifteen years of listening have not taught me that it is inferior to the ear of the author of *Twelfth Night*. The reader who heard the damage done, in my variation, to Pound's line—*So old Elkin had only one glory* —will be able to form his own opinion.

---

based upon a conventional oath of *personal* loyalty to the King made when Casement was knighted for services 'to the Crown' as a civil servant investigating atrocities in the Putomayo.

We write verse—was it Renoir, 'I paint with my penis'—we write verse with our ears; so this is important. Forming, animating, quelling his material, that ear is one of the main, weird facts of modern verse. It imposes upon the piteous stuff of the *Pisan Cantos* a 'distance' as absolute as upon the dismissal of the epigram just cited. The poet has listened to his life, so to speak, and he tells us that which he hears.

Both the personality-as-subject and the expressive personality are nearly uniform, I think, once they developed. In Yeats, in Eliot, we attend to reformations of personality. Not really in Pound; he is unregenerate. *'Toutes mes pièces datent de quinze ans,'* he quoted once with approval from a friend, and the contrast he draws between the life of the poet as it ought to be (or has been) and as it is, this contrast is perennial. But if this account of the poet's subject is correct, what can have concealed it from most even sympathetic and perceptive critics and readers? With regard to critics, two things, I believe. All the best critics of Pound's work themselves write verse, most of them verse indebted to Pound's, much of it heavily; they have been interested in craft, not personality and subject. Also they have been blinded, perhaps, by the notion of the 'impersonality' of the poet. This perverse and valuable doctrine, associated in our time with Mr. Eliot's name, was toyed with by Goethe and gets expression in Keats's insistence that the poet 'has no identity—he is continually in, for, and filling some other body.' For poetry of a certain mode (the dramatic) this is a piercing notion; for most other poetry, including Pound's, it is somewhat paradoxical, and may disfigure more than it enlightens. It hides motive, which persists. It fails to enable us to see, for instance, that the dominant source of inspiration in Keats's sonnet on Chapman's Homer is *antagonism,* his contempt for Pope and Pope's Homer. (This view, which I offer with due hesitation, is a development from an industrious and thoughtful biography of the sonnet by a British scholar in *Essays and Studies* for 1931.)

The reader is in one way more nearly right than the majority of critics. He is baffled by a heterogeneity of matter, as to which I shall have more to say in a moment, but he hears a personality in Pound's poetry. In fact, his hostility—we reach it at last—is based upon this. The trouble is that he hears the personality he expected to hear, rather than the one that is essentially there. He hears Pound's well-known prose personality, bellicose, programmatic, positive, and he resents it. Mr. Pound is partly responsible. This personality does exist in him, it is what he has lived with, and he can even write poetry with it, as we see in 'Sestina: Altaforte' and elsewhere early and late. A follower of Browning, he takes a keenly *active* view of poetry, and has, conceivably, a most imperfect idea both of just what his subject is and of what his expressive personality is like.

This personality is feline, supra-delicate, absorbed. If Browning made the fastest verse in English, Pound makes the slowest, the most discrete and suave. He once said of a story in *Dubliners* that it was something better than a story, it was 'a vivid waiting,' and the phrase yields much of his own quality. There is restlessness; but the art of the poet places itself, above all, immediately and mysteriously at the service of the passive and elegiac, the nostalgic. The true ascendancy of this personality over the other is suggested by a singular fact: the degree in which the mantic character is absent from his poetry. He looks ahead indeed, looks ahead eagerly, but he does not *feel* ahead; he feels back. (Since writing the sentence, I come on the phrase in Fenollosa, an impressive remark, 'The chief work of literary men in dealing with language, and of poets especially, lies in feeling back along the ancient lines of advance.') It is the poetry of a late craftsman; of an expatriate—

> Moaneth alway my mind's lust
> That I fare forth, that I afar hence
> Seek out a foreign fastness.   ('The Seafarer')

> Here we are, picking the first fern-shoots
> And saying: When shall we get back to our country?
> •   •   •   •   •
> Our sorrow is bitter, but we would not return to our
>   country.   (Cathay's first lines)

—of a failing culture. The personality is full already in 'The Return' from *Ripostes,* —return of the hunters, or literary men, for like others of Pound's poems this is a metaphor: those who in an earlier poem had cried

> 'Tis the white stag, Fame, we're ahunting,'

now come back illusionless.

From "The Poetry of Ezra Pound," *Partisan Review,* 16 (1949), 377-94.

MARGARET SCHLAUCH

The Anti-Humanism of Ezra Pound

ANOTHER SEQUENCE of two pages (p. 98 f.) is a kind of self-reproach for the sin of vanity. It is directed, however, not to the author alone, but to the whole human race:

> The ant's a centaur in his dragon world.
> Pull down thy vanity, it is not *man* [italics added]
> Made courage, or made order, or made grace,...

Man is here declared inferior to the lower orders of nature ("the green world") in artistic qualities,—but this is at bottom a comparison of incomparables. He is also declared inferior in attributes of moral choice ("courage"); and this means denying him the very attributes which make him proudly and uniquely human. Thus Ezra Pound achieves his value judgment. He says that non-human nature surpasses mankind in specifically human attributes. Nonsense again: contumelious nonsense....

The memories of Mr. Pound's past are, like his literary borrowings, inter-woven with impressions of the prisoners' camp where he composed them. Soldiers' speech, visual images, sensations of cold and rain obtrude themselves in the catalogues. There are comments on issues of war and peace. There are cries for pity. There is a direct statement that there are no righteous wars (p. 61), and an invective against all of them:

> woe to them that conquer with armies
> and whose only might is their power (p. 41).

This comes oddly from Mussolini's panegyrist, who vehemently supported the aggression of fascist Italy. And so we come to the major theme of the book, unified and carefully designed as it is.

The major theme. —This is the sordidness of cash; in particular, cash which represents interest on investments; still more specifically, interest drawn by Jewish bankers who drive the poor Gentiles into war:

> the yidd is a stimulant, and the goyim are cattle
> in gt/ proportion and go to saleable slaughter
> with the maximum of docility (p. 17).

Or, in polyglot style:

> po'eri di'aoli   [read dia'oli?]
> po'eri di'aoli sent to the slaughter
> Knecht gegen Knecht
> to the sound of the bumm drum, to eat remnants
>   for a userer's holiday to change the
> price of a currency
>   METATHEMENON [in Greek letters] (p. 40 f.);

"and to change the value of money, of the unit of money/ METATHEME-NON/ we are not yet out of *that* chapter" (p. 46); also: "the root stench being usura and METATHEMENON" (i.e., that which is changed) (p. 59); and most clearly here:

> and the two largest rackets are the alternation
>   of the value of money
> (of the unit of money   METATHEMENON TE TON
>   KRUMENON
>
> and usury @ 60   or lending
>   that which is made out of nothing . . . (p. 18).

The last phrase is important. It gives the medieval scholastic reason for objecting to interest: not because it results from the exploitation of human labor (the nature of which was of course not understood at the time), but because it appeared to violate nature in producing something *ex nihilo*. Pound's distaste, however, is revealed as demagogic many times. In phraseology, in design, and in the cheap tricks of juxtaposition it exemplifies fascist oratorical hocus-pocus. You attack Jewish and alien bankers and monopolists ("merrda for the monopolists/ the bastardly lot of 'em," p. 57; cf. the reference to Sir Montagu [Norman], p. 52), but never your own (in this instance, the fascist Italian), or ever the system that produces them. You attack the British empire—

> and in India the rate down to 18 per hundred
> but the local loan lice provided from imported bankers
> so the total interest sweated out of the Indian farmers
>   rose in Churchillian grandeur
> as when, and plus when, he returned to the putrid
>   gold standard (p. 4),—

but you do not attack the basis of imperialism as a whole, and you never, oh never, attack its fascist forms.

The omissions and the context make up the damning revelation of intention. The contexts are the essence of Pound's technique, as we have seen. Nowhere is it more cheaply employed than in these major passages.

Here is another example, frequently stressed. Since his adopted ideology compels Pound to besmirch all struggles for liberty, and the fraternal heroism engendered in democratic wars of defense, past and present, he undertakes to "debunk" the Battle of Salamis, since it has been a text-book example for ages of that kind of war. And the device? It is once more the juxtaposition of sordid cash with what claims to be great. We are reminded, with repetitious insistence, that "the fleet at Salamis [was] made with money lent by the state to the shipwrights" (p. 7 *et passim*). That is supposed to vilify the entire struggle of the Greeks to protect their homeland from the Persians.

Thus, as we end our analysis of techniques, we eventually find ourselves examining ideology. Nor could this be avoided. It was Mr. Pound who has-tened the juncture. He did not need to raise the issues just discussed; no one forced him to vilify what he did, while protecting *ex silentio* and otherwise the system which launched a program of genocide and aggressive wars. He could have written about his birds and sunsets and classical myths exclusively if he had so wished; but these are minor threads in his "warp and woof." *Pisan Cantos* is an anti-human document, convicted by the major themes it chooses to exploit.

And this leads us to the final condemnation. "Left" criticism has been rejected by some readers, even those abhorring fascism, because they claim that in the fullness of time the ideology of a poem becomes a matter of indifference. One can admire Homer and Dante and Milton, they say, without accepting their views of the universe, their local myths and theologies. But the question is not so simple as that. Though these comments may contain an element of truth, the only element they omit is the essential one. True it is that we don't accept Homer's anthropomorphic deities, and many of us differ with the precise schemes of Dante and Milton. But the essential resides in their grandiose and unprovincial symbolisms, which so rise above creed and dogma that they give us something of universal validity for all mens' aspirations. Much of Dante is easily translated into such universally valid terms quite apart from his theology. And the greatest kinship of all among them is their commitment to a construc-tive world view; a common belief in the dignity of man as a special and responsible creature in the "green world" of nature; a belief in his worthiness to be fostered into something still more brave and generous and noble than he has ever been in the past. His failings may be presented, with deep and justified loathing for their ugliness, but his fundamental nature is not be-smirched.

To place Pound beside these great figures, and claim for him a special immunity because he is supposed to be of their clan, is the most vilifying of all juxtapositions. Only, in this instance, the tables are turned and it is Pound himself who is cheapened. This is not merely a political and social judgment; it is a humane one. Great poetry has something to do, they say, with the greatness of the human spirit. And Ezra Pound is anti-human as well as anti-humanistic.

From "The Anti-Humanism of Ezra Pound," *Science and Society,* 13 (Sum-mer 1949), 258-69.

ROBERT LANGBAUM

Ezra Pound's Dramatic Monologues

POUND ACTUALLY makes dramatic monologues of his paraphrases from the personal utterances of ancient poets by intruding into them a modern consciousness. By employing an idiom and a tone so unmistakably contemporary as to give us an historical view of the utterance that the ancient poet could not himself have had, Pound uses the ancient poet as the speaker of a dramatic monologue. For he projects himself into the ancient poet's role, using him as a mouthpiece to dramatize an idea of the poet's time and civilization suitable to Pound's modern purpose.[1] This is the same historical point of view which Eliot achieves with mythological analogies in *The Waste Land* —with his use, for example, of Tiresias as speaker in a poem with a contemporary setting and in contemporary idiom; and which Yeats achieves with art symbols—with the mosaic settings of the *Byzantium* poems, and with those carved Chinamen in *Lapis Lazuli* who manage to convey the sense of fallen civilizations:

> Their eyes mid many wrinkles, their eyes,
> Their ancient, glittering eyes, are gay.

The historical meaning that emerges is beyond what Yeats' Chinamen could know of themselves, just as a specifically twentieth-century meaning emerges from the cadences of Pound's Propertius:

> A Trojan and adulterous person came to Menelaus
>   under the rites of hospitium,
> And there was a case in Colchis, Jason and that woman
>   in Colchis;
> And besides, Lynceus,
>   you were drunk

or from the juxtapositions in Pound's Rihaku:

> The paired butterflies are already yellow with August
> Over the grass in the West garden;

1. "If one can really penetrate the life of another age, one is penetrating the life of one's own. . . . [Pound] is much more modern, in my opinion, when he deals with Italy and Provence, than when he deals with modern life." (Eliot's Introduction to Pound's *Selected Poems*, London: Faber and Faber, 1935, pp. xii-xiii.)

They hurt me. I grow older.
If you are coming down through the narrows of the river Kiang,
Please let me know beforehand,
And I will come out to meet you
                              As far as Cho-fu-Sa.

Pound projects a similar point of view in his original dramatic monologue, *The Tomb at Akr Çaar,* in which a soul makes love to its mummified body, for whose return to life it has been waiting, lingering in the tomb, these five millennia. Integral to the meaning is our modern awareness that the monologue takes place as the tomb is about to be opened, that this is the five-thousand-year-old situation the archaeologists will break into.

In these historical poems, the extraordinary moral position and the extraordinary emotion become historical phenomena. The past becomes, in other words, a means for achieving another extraordinary point of view. Since the past is understood in the same way that we understand the speaker of the dramatic monologue, the dramatic monologue is an excellent instrument for projecting an historical point of view. For the modern sense of the past involves, on the one hand, a sympathy for the past, a willingness to understand it in its own terms as different from the present; and on the other hand it involves a critical awareness of our own modernity. In the same way, we understand the speaker of the dramatic monologue by sympathizing with him, and yet by remaining aware of the moral judgment we have suspended for the sake of understanding. The combination of sympathy and judgment makes the dramatic monologue suitable for expressing all kinds of extraordinary points of view, whether moral, emotional or historical—since sympathy frees us for the widest possible range of experience, while the critical reservation keeps us aware of how far we are departing. The extraordinary point of view is characteristic of all the best dramatic monologues, the pursuit of experience in all its remotest extensions being the genius of the form.

From *The Poetry of Experience* (New York: Random House, 1957), pp. 94-96.

FORREST READ

The Pattern of the *Pisan Cantos*

LIKE DANTE, Pound undertakes in the *Pisan Cantos* a spiritual journey: in his word, the periplum. The periplum is the letter of Pound's poem, the journey undertaken by that sensibility which is the persona. And it is the consciousness that bears the burden of the allegory, the spirit on the way to resolution. From time to time Pound speaks directly and consciously: to register immediate emotion; to evaluate the persona's state in its periplum; to mark progress toward the ultimate goal of redemption and resolution. A reader of the poem can easily verify this separation by taking note of the passages in which Pound discusses his own state of mind or spirit.

The periplum of the persona passes through three general areas of experience. First, that of Pound's own past and present: memories of his youth in the United States, of his friends and fellow artists in Europe, of his travels, and of his prison-camp confinement. This sphere also includes the states of western civilization as Pound has known it, and records historical events and personages: in the present, Europe as the "broken anthill." The fragments are infernal in their subjection to time, but as components of Pound's being they are being pressed by his sensibility to redemption. The image of Europe is the prison camp itself, and Pound's confinement there is symbolic of civilization in a period of chaos. Civilization must be rebuilt by a reordering of values; but the reordering will take meaning only from the quality of mind and spirit within which it occurs: hence the need for redemption, which is carried out by purification of the will.

The need for redemption leads to the second realm, that of the natural world which surrounds the camp. Visible nature is the self-renewing factor, the flux; like the signs of the zodiac in the frescoes and like paradiso terrestre, it is the symbol of the timeless process which animates it. The gods and goddesses are symbols of the permanent paradisal energies which move nature. Pound-as-persona contemplates the world of nature as the source of possible redemption; and, by purification of the will as the path by which he can achieve harmony with nature, he prepares himself for revelation.

Revelation takes place in the third realm, that of ancient wisdom: folk, classical, Christian, and Confucian. Permanent wisdom is the result of past revelations of the harmony which exists in the process of the universe; and these revelations, however fossilized, make up the tradition which is pressing on men in the present and will continue to press on them in the future. But while the persona ranges through the realm of timeless truth, ancient wisdom must be made new in the consciousness as it reorders the lost city of spiritual order.

What Pound seeks in his dual role as experiencer and ordering consciousness is a synthesis of the three realms: of his past and present, including the world of time in which they existed and exist; of the natural world, which contains the unarticulated process of the universe; and of timeless guides to action which have been won from unarticulated nature. The formed synthesis will then give him identity and offer a guide to future action.

But making himself new does not itself guarantee the epic resolution of harmony with the universe or revelation of the mystery. For the persona it is the intensity with which the sensibility conceives, and for the consciousness it is the purification of the will, that prepare the epic hero for the reception of enlightenment: or consciously-known harmony with "the process," as Pound calls it, of the universe. In the *Pisan Cantos* there is a clear movement toward ordering of the spirit and creation of forms which imitate the rhythm of the process, so that after the will has been purified grace is breathed into those forms and revelation and union take place. . . .

Such is the soul of the movement: pursuit of form in the persona until metamorphosis is stayed; purification of will in the consciousness; and articulation as persona and consciousness merge in the clarity of revelation and union. While Dante's *Commedia* moves in a geographical continuum characteristic of medieval cosmology, Pound's movement takes place in quanta, characteristic of modern physics. Thus Pound works toward a focus by an expenditure of emotional and poetic energy, and when focus fails, reinaugurates the movement from a new plane of purification: not at the level of attempted focus itself, but commencing with the same materials in a more regenerated persona and consciousness.

By moving in a continuum Dante gives the impression of a separation of his realms. But as a matter of fact he uses symbolic similarity to suggest their interdependence, for they are root, leaf, and flower of his spiritual experience and cannot exist without each other. Thus there is symbolic copresence in the structure of the fosse, the mountain, and the spheres, which culminate in the three respective interdependent symbols, Satan, Eden, and the rose. And all three exist in the continuity of God's will, which permeates the universe. Pound, on the other hand, by using quantum movement, maintains infernal, purgatorial, and paradisal principles throughout. After all, he does not have any ready-made symbolic system like Dante's. Thus Canto LXXIV marks the chaotic state of his Inferno, and Cantos LXXVI-LXXX are the creative movements through Purgatorio toward paradiso terrestre, achieved when metamorphosis is held in the England lyrics. In this respect, the quantum movements toward redemption take place along linear scales of emotion. But at the same time the persona is making a journey among the experiences out of which the consciousness is being formed, and is seeking a new ordering of the three realms: of self (as prisoner of time, infernal); of nature (as time redeemed in its harmony with the process, purgatorial); and of ancient wisdom (as revelation of the process in the human mind, paradisal). The persona records and reforms the elements into new complexes; these complexes manifest the states of sensibility which obtain as the consciousness regenerates itself. Within the linear movements of the consciousness, therefore, there is continuous relative movement among the elements of experience.

The structure of Pound's movements can be charted as follows:

Canto LXXIV: Undirected spiritual chaos (Inferno)

Canto LXXV: Rest and relief (as in antepurgatorio, Casella's song to Dante); and presage of form.

Cantos LXXVI-LXXVII: Broken dual movement; the first canto ending on condemnation of war, the second seeking focus after "mind come to plenum when nothing more will go into it".

Cantos LXXVIII-LXXIX: Second broken dual movement; the first canto again ending on condemnation of war, the second with sustainment which slips to metamorphosis but establishes formative affection affirmed for creative action.

Canto LXXX: Integral creative movement which reconciles sensibility and nature, affirms purification of will and preparation for resolution and revelation.

Canto LXXXI: Revelation as recreated self is articulated in the consciousness.

Canto LXXXII: Impact of revelation and fundamental basis of existence expressed "past metaphor"; "man, earth: two halves of the tally"; immersion in "fluid ΧΘΟΝΟΣ"; end of periplum.

Canto LXXXIII: Articulation of wisdom, union with the process, of which Pound has become consciously a part.

Canto LXXXIV: Epilogue.

Pound's epic movement issues, then, in his creation of a new self out of materials of the past and present, out of achieved harmony with the process, and out of union with the rhythms of the process. The entire movement beginning with Canto LXXVI, after exit from the shut-in world of Canto LXXIV and the restful pause of Canto LXXV, lives as formation of the plant whose growth has moved from the seeds to the ultimate flower. And in the allegory Pound becomes a surrogate for modern man in a modern form of epic. . . .

In the *Pisan Cantos,* however, Pound develops a full sense of responsibility for himself and for the western civilization from which he had previously isolated himself so vituperatively. His self-examination becomes through its sincerity the self-examination of us all; and its intensity fuses himself, western culture, Confucius, and the process of nature into a significant unity. It is that intensity itself which gives birth to the force of dramatic tension between persona and consciousness. This is not to say that the *Pisan Cantos* succeed only because they are personal. Rather Pound uses himself as a metaphor just as Dante did, and the very simplicity of that structure gives the poem life. It is difficult to see as urgent structure for the entire poem either Pound's suggestions of recurring themes; parallels to the *Odyssey* and the *Commedia;* or Mr.

Kenner's contention that the poem is successfully organized by metaphor, "an acute intuition of . . . similarity and dissimilarity . . . actions, passions, places, times, blocks of experience . . . set in relation."

As for values on which to base action, which epic generates, Pound has made much of Dante's "hierarchy of values" controlled into order by "directio voluntatis," translated by Pound as "Rightness of choice of an end is secured by virtue." But the hierarchy of values Dante created came from a sensibility that was not only trying to create such values, but also to reconstitute a shattered self. These two processes moving inseparably together give the *Commedia* a character of inevitability and create the illusion that choice is independent of personal virtue: that the universe was indeed created by and is subject to God's will, not Dante's, and that the values presented lie deep in the nature of man and the universe. Such inevitability is absent from the *Cantos*, except in flashes, until the Pisan group. There that same sense of a true and significant experiencing of the human condition sustains Pound's epic movement and makes us believe in it and accept it for our own. The fragmentized quality becomes "right," in that it reflects the pulverization and reconstruction of the self in an urgent context; and the fragments, embedded as they are in an experiencing persona and a developing consciousness, are controlled by drama, not by association. Paradiso is in the earlier parts of the *Pisan Cantos,* as Pound says, "spezzato"; but as the poem evolves it becomes progressively more ordered until, when it is articulated, Paradiso is integral.

From "The Pattern of the *Pisan Cantos," The Sewanee Review,* 65 (1957), 400-419.

EDITH SITWELL

A Preface to Ezra Pound

EZRA POUND is one of the greatest living poets.

The *Cantos* included in this book are of the highest interest technically, as well as because of the great beauty of their imagery. Let us take this passage, from *Canto II;*

> And poor old Homer blind, blind, as a bat,
> Ear, ear for the sea-surge, murmur of old men's voices:
> "Let her go back to the ships,
> Back among Grecian faces, lest evil come on our own,
> Evil and further evil, and a curse cursed on our children,
> Moves, yes she moves like a goddess
> And has the face of a god
>   and the voice of Schoeney's daughters,
> And doom goes with her in walking,
> Let her go back to the ships,
>   Back among Grecian voices."

In the sound, in the echo of the second one-syllabled word "sea-surge," of "murmur of old men's voices," we are given an evocation of the fact that the sea-surge is immemorially old, has an immemorable wisdom echoing through time. The "sea-surge" and the "murmur of old men's voices" are then separate entities, but they have come together, and are one, or at least are scarcely separate in the ear of age and wisdom. The whole passage has the movement, the majestic sound of waves breaking in all their different splendor: "And doom goes with her in walking."

In that great line we have the whole sound, gathered throughout the ages, of the sea.

Part of the magic conveying the sound of the sea is obtained by the echoes which come from time to time; the sound of "surge," for instance, is echoed, three lines further on, by the less long sound of "curse," repeated twice, like the sound of a wave gathering itself and spreading outwards: "Evil and further evil, and a curse cursed on our children"; and the sound of "moves" in the line "Moves, yes she moves like a goddess" has, after the interval of two lines, the far deeper echo of "doom," a sound which contains all the hollowness and reverberation of the sea-depths. There is an echo, too, at the end of the lines:

and the voice of Schoeney's *daughters,*
And doom goes with her in *walking.*

The whole sound is that of the sea, with all the sea's depth.

The first two *Cantos* are a magnificent achievement. The wide stretch of the sea, the scarcely perceptible movement of the ripples, the clear sea airs, are all conveyed by means of the fluctuating lengths of the opening lines of the first *Canto,* and by the shifting of the first accent from the first syllable to the second syllable of the line; and by the fact also that the second line is only part of a phrase and is therefore part of a terrific sweeping movement, with a pause wherein the wind gathers.

The first *Canto's* first line finds us sailing over a sea . . . and if there is a more terrific sweeping onward of movement (that is yet perfectly smooth) to be found in all English poetry, I have yet to find it.

A small wave comes in the middle of the sixth line, with the faint stresses, placed in immediate juxtaposition, of "out onward," breaks beneath the ship, and the ship sweeps on again.

Both these opening *Cantos* have the most strangely accurate, sharp, acutely observed visual impressions, like the portrait of the seal in the second *Canto.*

The movement of the ship seems to grow faster, in the second *Canto,* with the shortening of the lines, and with the tight effect of the one-syllabled ending of some of the lines, followed by the strong accent on the first syllable of the next line, alternating with the loosening caused by certain feminine endings:

> Ship stock fast in sea-swirl
> Ivy upon the oars, King Pentheus,
>   grapes with no seed but sea-foam,
> Ivy in scupper-hole.

Indeed, the whole of these two *Cantos* may be said to be a miracle of the transfusion of sense into sound; or rather, of the fusion of the two.

In the first part of the second *Canto,* the first accent of the lines shifts its place perpetually, though the movement is not elaborately contrapuntal.

The reason for the more embodied and hard-outlined movement, for its condensation, may be found in the lines:

> void air taking pelt.
> Lifeless air become sinewed.

In this miraculous poetry Pound, by some enchantment, fuses the sense of the beasts with the sense of the oncoming tempest.

The rhythms have an extraordinary variety, a lovely flexibility and inevitability that is sometimes like the "feline leisure of panthers," or like the fluctuating, flowing, waving sound of the airs coming from some immortal sea. The echoes indeed, and the sounds that originate them, vary, as do the sounds and echoes in certain of Milton's songs, from sea air to sea air, from wave to wave, as the beauty of the line lengthens and then runs back again.

At the end of the second *Canto* we have an example of this consummate power of variation. For after the plunging forward of the ship, after the embodying of the beasts, beasts with fur as thick and dark as clouds, with movements like sinewed lightning, in an air "without tempest," we have this sudden dew-laden peace that is not the result of association alone, but also of the lengthening of the line, the scarcely perceptible beat of the accents, and of what is practically an absence of caesura:

> And we have heard the fauns chiding Proteus
> > in the smell of hay under the olive-trees,
> And the frogs singing against the fauns
> > in the half-light.
> And . . .

Amid the sad darkness of the mind shown in many of the *Cantos* not included here, the splendor of the passage quoted is amongst the most wonderful poetry that has been written in our time.

From *The Atlantic Book of British and American Poetry* (Boston: Little, Brown, 1958), pp. 993-95.

HUGH KENNER

The Broken Mirrors
and the Mirror of Memory

THE TITLE of the 1909 *Personae*, Pound's earliest collection of verse to achieve general circulation, implies not merely masks but a man donning them. It is the first of a long sequence of efforts on his part to draw our attention to the status of the poetic process itself as the central drama of his poetry. He will not have us think of him as a medium in which things happen, nor yet as a poet-hero striding and declaiming before backdrops of his own design. He will not, in fact, have us think of him at all: but he will ensure our awareness of his existence, exploring, voyaging, selecting, gathering experiences into a mind in which toward the close of his magnum opus they remain like Wagadu's City, "indestructible." The operations of this mind afford the dramatic continuity of *The Cantos*, but we do not always hear the unmistakably personal tone by which it announces its presence. As a personality, it makes strategic entrances and withdrawals. As a poetic agent, it is never absent for an instant. At the beginning of the poem the personality is in abeyance. Our attention is focused on Odysseus. We are not aware that a modern poet is telling the story: this Odysseus remains Homer's.

This commerce of the old and the new slips into the scheme of the poem with an unobtrusiveness so precise that a new reader is unlikely for some time to grasp its thematic weight. We have grown accustomed to watching the modern poet in the act of wresting his materials out of their own contexts into the dramatic contexts he provides for them, and when we see that happening— for example, in *The Waste Land* —we feel assured that the man is properly about his business, and attend with vigilance. Pound's way, however, is to await with a vigilance of his own the exact events that will enter his purposes without modification; the result is an undisturbed surface which, as Eliot remarked of Ben Jonson's, "reflects only the lazy reader's fatuity." Hence the appearance Canto I presents of a brilliant paraphrase of some lines of Homer's, with a few enigmatic phrases tacked on at the end: a bit of Homer pasted onto the title page of Pound's album, to preface the bits of Ovid, Cavalcanti, Sordello, Sappho, Confucius, and Lincoln Steffens.

This effect is the liability of a carefully calculated risk. Pound is determined to dispel at the start the notion that the things in his poem are symbols: that he says what he seems to be saying only as a way of saying something else. Canto I is not an elaborate metaphor. Nevertheless it is not "just Homer." Such a phrase, for one thing, is impertinent. Homer is not just a Greek document, he contains, incarnates, a paideuma. And the Canto, informed by that paideuma, *does* a great deal more than at first glance it *is*, and ultimately is what it does—something surprisingly comprehensive. Among other functions, it is one half of a parable for the complete Poundian doctrine of the creative act (Canto II is the other half).

In Canto I we have ritual, magic, homage to forerunners, and ghosts supplied with blood which enables them to speak in the present. The journey to the homes of the dead must be the first enterprise of the artist in quest of what is called in *Hugh Selwyn Mauberley* "his true Penelope." Piety to his forerunners is an element in this journey. The Elpenor who fell off Circe's ladder after a night of "abundant wine" reminds us of

> how Johnson (Lionel) died
> By falling from a high stool in a pub

and it is a pleasant coincidence that Odysseus' stele for his lost crewman ("A man of no fortune and with a name to come") has its parallel in Pound's preface to his selection of Lionel Johnson's poems. The blood for the ghosts is an analogue for translation; he brings them blood, and they speak anew with their own voices. Appropriately, translation is the mode of this Canto; with the aid of a Renaissance crib, Homer's Greek acquires the blood of Pound's English. It is not only the oldest surviving poetry in the Greek language, it is also, Pound thinks, the oldest part of Homer's subject matter: "The Nekuia shouts aloud that it is *older* than the rest . . . hintertime . . . *not* Praxiteles, not Athens of Pericles, but Odysseus" (*Letters*, p. 274). So it goes into the oldest available English, the rhythms and locutions of the Anglo-Saxon *Seafarer*. The whole makes a great piece of twentieth-century verse; and at the end of it the vision of a goddess is vouchsafed:

> Venerandam,
> In the Cretan's phrase, with the golden crown, Aphrodite.

She is the archetype of what comes out of the flux, and she manifests herself briefly to reward these labors.

Pound is always aware in this way of a drama implicit in the very application of words to things. In Canto XXIII we find him at work translating a bit of Greek—

> With the sun in a golden cup
> and going toward the low fords of ocean

—in the company of scientists not spinning abstractions but working toward useful results, Gemisto preferring explicit political actions to a dispute about the procession of the Holy Ghost, and Psellos declaring that the intellect is God's fire, omniform. This Canto, like the first, ends with the birth of Aphrodite:

> and saw then, as of waves taking form,
> As the sea, hard, a glitter of crystal,
> And the waves rising but formed, holding their form.
> No light reaching through them.

Something formed and permanent emerges from the flux of experience; this is a conquest over chaos requiring a technique as exact as M. Curie's scientific training.

Of the three long poems Pound wrote before embarking on *The Cantos*, the earliest, "Near Perigord" (1915), while it is the least impressive, most repays exegetical investigation. It is an elaborate parable of the poetic enterprise.

Bertrans de Born, one of Pound's first personae, wrote, as everyone knows, a canzone assembling the perfections of seven Provençal beauties to make an "ideal lady" in lieu of one named Maent who had turned him out. The task Pound sets himself in "Near Perigord" is to educe from documentary fragments a satisfying image of Bertrans, his selfhood and his world, so as to answer the question whether the poem is what it seems to be, an expression of thwarted love, or whether it is a political maneuver designed to flatter the seven beauties, set their lords at strife with Maent's lord whose castle menaced his line of communications, and win his jongleur a spy's access to their strongholds. There is nothing for Pound to work with but chance facts, and facts are suggestive but impenetrable: anecdotes about Bertrans' character, observations on the layout of the terrain, precedents for singing love when you mean war. The first part of the poem canvasses the facts and ends where it began:

> What is Sir Bertrans' singing?
> Maent, Maent, and yet again Maent,
> Or war and broken heaumes and politics?

In the second part we "try fiction"; three or four scenes visualized in the mind's eye, hypothetical visions groping toward the living truth:

> Let us say we see
> En Bertrans, a tower room at Hautefort,
> Sunset, the ribbon-like road lies, in red cross-light,
> Southward toward Montaignac, and he bends at a table
> Scribbling, swearing between his teeth; by his left hand
> Lie little strips of parchment covered over,
> Scratched and erased with *al* and *ochaisos*.
> Testing his list of rhymes, a lean man? Bilious?
> With a red straggling beard?
> And the green cat's eye lifts toward Montaignac.

This is plausible enough, and it is also an achievement in vivid re-creation, but we do not know if it is what a visitor would have seen, circa 1190. Nor would a contemporary's testimony necessarily have been helpful. The section ends with a pair of contemporaries, Arnaut Daniel and Richard Plantagenet, discussing the problem after Bertrans' death:

"You knew the man."
"*You* knew the man."
"I am an artist, you have tried both métiers."
"You were born near him."
"Do we know our friends?"
"Say that he saw the castles, say that he loved Maent!"
"Say that he loved her, does it solve the riddle?"

Those who "knew" him were as baffled as we who know only documents. The image of Bertrans is still eluding us. Suddenly, out of this chaos, Dante Alighieri educes a form:

> *Surely I saw, and still before my eyes*
> *Goes on that headless trunk, that bears for light*
> *Its own head swinging, gripped by the dead hair,*
> *And like a swinging lamp that says, "Ah me!*
> *I severed men, my head and heart*
> *Ye see here severed, my life's counterpart."*

This, not anything recoverable from documents or from the testimony of any acquaintance however intimate, is the image of Bertrans de Born that has persisted for six hundred years. It does not directly assist our present enquiries, but it is unchallengeably real. The one reality that no discussion shakes is evinced by art. The living Bertrans perplexed his contemporaries; what we can learn of him perplexes us. Fact is grist for guesses. But no commentary can bring further light to what Dante has done in these lines, and no inquisition embarrass it.

The introduction of this pasage from Dante suddenly catalyzes the poem Pound is writing; into the anxious climate of research into enigmatic life it brings the cool steady air of Art, and incites the recollection that Bertrans' canzone was a work of art, before it occurred to anyone to treat it as a document. Since it is a work of art, its focus is on its subject Maent, and the final portion of Pound's poem moves swiftly to an image of Maent herself:

> She who could never live save through one person,
> She would could never speak save to one person,
> And all the rest of her a shifting change,
> A broken bundle of mirrors . . . !

Bertrans' canzone, in other words, is literally accurate homage: Maent herself, like the lady in the canzone, *was* a collection of fragments. Perhaps it was a love-poem. Perhaps it sang of war. Perhaps it had this or that personal motiva-

tion. But preeminently, it was imitation in the Aristotelian sense: an arrangement of words and images corresponding to the mode of being possessed by
the subject. Our researches via fact and fiction were inconclusive because we
were looking at the poet and not at what he was writing about: a woman not
yet "awakened," with brilliant surfaces but no center. Pound imagines her
response to Bertrans' declaration of love:

> "Why do you love me? Will you always love me?
> But I am like the grass, I cannot love you."
> Or "Love, and I love, and love you,
> And hate your mind, not *you,* your soul, your hands."

"Like the grass," having no personal center from which to direct her affections;
or "I love, and love you, / And hate your mind," loving therefore like a
Provençal Emma Bovary a shadowy Bertrans, not the man himself.

Bertrans' paradoxical triumph, that of an artist, was to bring form out of
such a flux; the form was not that of Aphrodite, but that of a composite lady.
It was—and is—the form of what was there. Pound attempted something
similar in his "Portrait d'une Femme," an image of a lady whose mind is a
Sargasso Sea:

> and yet,
> For all this sea-horde of deciduous things,
> Strange woods half-sodden, and new brighter stuff:
> In the slow float of differing light and deep,
> No! there is nothing! In the whole and all,
> Nothing that's quite your own.
> Yet this is you.

This is the same sort of woman as Maent; she exists only as a sort of nodal
point in the flux, where "ideas, old gossip, oddments of all things" have
collected. Superficially, the poem has nothing whatever in common with
Bertrans' canzone: Maent is an accumulation of feminine perfections, not a sort
of junkshop. The woman of Pound's poem, however, is the early twentieth-
century London incarnation of this persistent human type: the "broken bundle
of mirrors." She reflects fragments of the events around her, and her appropriate imagery is that of the romantic deliquescence, ambergris, mandrakes, redo-
lent curiosa, as different as possible from the Provençal crispness reflected by
her predecessor Maent.

What Pound has done in the poem, and what he implies Bertrans did in
the canzone, is define a person who incarnates the flux itself. To define
something, to coerce the motions of the sea of experience into a form, is the
first business of the artist. This is the meaning of Aphrodite's birth from the
sea foam. It is also the business of the person, and some people manage to
imprint themselves unmistakably on the events by which they are surrounded.
Sigismundo Malatesta was one of these. It is because Malatesta and Pound have

similar objectives that Pound has presented Malatesta, in Cantos VIII-XI, through the medium of the circumambient events themselves. The man's personality emerges as powerfully from the miscellany of documents in *The Cantos* as it emerged from the welter of events chronicled by the documents. This is imitation once more; Malatesta has the same sort of intelligible existence in the poem that he had in fact.

This recalls us to Canto II, the theme of which is form out of flux. By form is meant intelligible form, like Aphrodite visible to the mind's eye. This Canto has, to be sure, a good deal to do with metamorphosis as well as with the sea; but the point about metamorphosis is that it implies a change of matter, not really of form. The swimming nymph transformed into a growth of coral is still the same person, rigid, brittle, and uncompliant. Her intelligible form, if not the physical form which is merely a silhouette of matter, remains what it was. But in her new state we see more easily what she is. This Canto polarizes Canto I. If translation—recreation—is one lobe of the poetic act, the eduction of forms is the other. The two are not antithetical: Canto II contains a translated passage (from Ovid), and Canto I performs a metamorphosis—Greek to Latin to English.

Canto II opens with four cryptic lines which condense the themes canvassed in "Near Perigord": .

> Hang it all, Robert Browning,
> there can be but the one "Sordello."

"Sordello" the poem, like Dante's image of Bertrans, is art and hence final, defying modification, despite the questions that still haunt the documents Browning worked from.

> But Sordello, and my Sordello?

But Sordello the living man, whose heart, despite the finality of Browning's poem, remains for us strangers a dark forest? And Pound's Sordello—the image of the living man that forms in Pound's mind and is not identical with the one that formed in Browning's?

> Lo Sordels si fo di Mantovana

This is a nugget of documentary fact. It is part of the documentary chaos Browning sloughed off in educing his hero. But it also typifies the sort of irreducible testimony Pound in pursuit of his own objectives is determined not to slough off; the sort of thing through which, rather than in spite of which, Pound is to present his own Renaissance hero, Sigismundo. People are not animated formulae: they exist amid a process which they mirror even in contending with it. Maent who was a broken bundle of mirrors, incarnate flux, is the extreme case of what every human being manifests. A man cannot be separated from his acts, nor acts from context, nor either from the traces they have left in document and oral tradition. These latter—the historian's "sources"—are in their very discreteness analogues of what they attest to. Browning was not occupied as Pound is with historical truth; for instance he altered—Pound says "with perfect right"[1]—the ending of Sordello's story to suit his own purpose. His way of making historical men and women real was not unlike that of Walter Scott—his imagination, spurred by historians' hints which he disregarded when they proved inconvenient or intractable, conceived dramatic characters, more or less in the image of Robert Browning, which were then projected onto a colorfully drawn background. The kind of "truth" Browning can claim is dramatic and psychological. Pound however wants his poem about history to be historically true—that is, an image of how things really happen, presented in terms of what happens in Pound's mind when he considers the records. Hence his distrust of Browning's or the school-of-Macaulay historians' kind of abstraction from fact. Things that really happened are also more interesting and complex than anything he can imagine. So his poetic achievement—his Aphrodite—is not to be a swimmer stepping out of the ocean but a crystallization into form of the flux itself. . . .

The key to Pound's method throughout *The Cantos* is his conviction that the things the poet sees in the sea of events are really there. They are not "creations" of his. Similarly, the values registered in the poem are not imported and affirmed by the poet, but discerned by him in the record of human experience. They are literally *there* to be discovered; it is not a twentieth-century poet-moralist, nor a consciousness colored by the shards of American Christianity, that puts them there. They are not even values created by Confucius or Erigena or Malatesta or anyone else. Their origin is not human, but divine. In the words of a formulation that comes very late in the poem,

                    it is not man
        Made courage, or made order, or made grace.

This brings us to the gods, who are the archetypal forms. "A god," Pound wrote thirty-five years ago, "is an eternal state of mind"; he is manifest "when the states of mind take form." This sounds as though the gods were human creations; but Pound warns us in *Pavannes* that the word "eternal" is to be taken literally:

            Are all eternal states of mind gods?
            We consider them so to be.
            Are all durable states of mind gods?
            They are not.   (p. 23)

Anything originally human is at best merely durable; the eternal state of mind has an eternal object. One thing that fitted the poets of the nineties to be crewmen of Pound-Odysseus was their conviction that certain supernatural types recurred. The great postulate, in fact the great cliché, of their poetry is

1. *Pavannes, and Divisions* (New York, 1918), p. 171.

the permanence of hypostatized Beauty, the cruel mistress of the artist. Pound opens his anthology *Profile* with Arthur Symons's "Modern Beauty":

> I am Yseult and Helen, I have seen
> Troy burn, and the most loving knight lie dead.
> The world has been my mirror, time has been
> My breath upon the glass

This goddess, like her polar opposite, the woman who is a broken bundle of mirrors, has her characteristic incarnation in every great period of art. Whenever she turns up in Pound's poetry we can identify her by her eyes. In the fourteenth century she is the "Merciles Beauté" to whom Chaucer wrote,

> Your eyen two wol sleye me sodenly
> I may the beauté of hem nat susteyne   (Canto LXXXI)

In the fifteenth century she is the Venus of Jacopo del Sellaio, of whom Pound writes in an early poem, "The Picture":

> The eyes of this dead lady speak to me.   (*Personae*, p. 73)

In the nineteenth century, when the arts themselves partake of a tepid and uncertain vitality, she is the woman in *Hugh Selwyn Mauberley* with the "yeux glauques" and the "half-ruin'd face" who sat for Rossetti and Burne-Jones:

> The Burne-Jones cartons
> Have preserved her eyes
>
> Thin, like brook-water,
> With a vacant gaze
>
> Questing and passive   (*Personae*, p. 192)

In 1945 she is a barefoot girl, "la scalza," who says "Io son' la luna" —I am the moon.

> la scalza   :   Io son' la luna
> and they have broken my house[2]   (Canto LXXXVI)

This new incarnation of the eternal Beauty is identified with Jacopo's vision and Arthur Symons's ruinous supernatural mistress near the end of Canto LXXX, where the moon-girl[3] rides

---

2. For other allusions, see *The Pisan Cantos*, pp. 16, 21, 30, 31, and 78.
3. This is the barefooted moon-girl transfigured. "La scalza" is Cythera (Aphrodite) incarnate in Pisa, as the "pastorella dei suini" (*The Pisan Cantos*, pp. 38, 118) is Circe.

with the veil of faint cloud before her
Κύθηρα δεινὰ as a leaf borne in the current
pale eyes as if without fire

and in the next Canto finally brings "new subtlety of eyes" into the Pisan tent.
The continually reincarnated goddess is herself the supreme form won out of flux; but Pound goes beyond the nineties in not being content with doing her elegiac homage. The point of adducing her here is to illustrate Pound's belief in her actual existence. If the word "belief" makes for epistemological embarrassment, it can be qualified with quotation marks; at any rate, a faith that the flux contains intelligible forms not simply projected there by the observer underlies the whole enterprise of *The Cantos*. The details of the poem, as we began by remarking, look so casual because Pound is determined not to intensify them by the pressure of superimposed meanings; his objective, in which he succeeds often enough to make the work cohere, is to find the scenes, persons, incidents, and quotations that will release into the poem without coercion the meanings they intrinsically contain. What he is writing about is, finally, human intelligence and the direction of the human will amid the events of history. The difficulty is that as the pressure cannot be separated from the water, so these forces can be perceived and discussed only in terms of the events they combat or animate. Only artists incarnate their intelligence and will in works that live on after them, and while artists are "the antennae of the race," the means of the good life are won for most men by rulers whose work dies when the tradition of their personal intelligence has left it. Pound's analogy in *Jefferson and/or Mussolini* between the statesman and the artist is well known. Both are known through their works. But the artist's works are indisputably *there,* the statesman's, being cut in the unstable material of events themselves, need to be elucidated with a careful eye to the author's character and intention. Bertrans de Born, we can now see, was both artist and man of action, and in one instance operated in both métiers with a single work. Pound closed the inquiry in "Near Perigord" by considering the canzone as a work of art and so an image of its subject; this does not really answer the question about Bertrans' ulterior intentions at all, since there is no reason why a poem could not be a self-contained work of art and also an instrument of policy. It is not the final insight of "Near Perigord" but the whole poem itself that disposes of that question. Pound sees no reason for supposing that aesthetic completeness cuts a work off from action.

From "The Broken Mirrors and the Mirror of Memory," *Motive and Method in the Cantos of Ezra Pound,* edited by Lewis Leary (New York: Columbia Univ. Press, 1954), pp. 3-32.

M. L. ROSENTHAL

Ezra Pound: The Poet as Hero

EXCITEMENT ATTENDS almost all Ezra Pound's prose and poetry—the excitement of the man himself, his urgency and cantankerousness and virtuosity.
Also, he has *authority*. In part this is the irritating authority of the self-
appointed leader, yet it is indisputable. One sees it in the reminiscences of his
oldest friends, still full of mingled admiration and resentment. 'An uncomfort-
ably tensed, nervously straining, jerky, reddish brown young American,' says
Wyndham Lewis, describing Pound's arrival in London in his mid-twenties.
'He had no wish to *mix;* he just wanted to *impress.*' For the British, as for his
own countrymen, he was 'an unassimilable and aggressive stranger.' Still, the
authority was there despite the hostile response; he stood for the most rigorous
poetic dedication, and the best writers were likely to recognize this fact.
William Carlos Williams records one such recognition:

> He knew of Yeats slightly while in America but to my knowledge did
> not become thoroughly acquainted with Yeats' work until he went to
> London in 1910. There a strange thing took place. He gave Yeats a hell
> of a bawling out for some of his inversions and other archaisms of style
> and, incredibly, Yeats turned over all his manuscripts to the moment to
> Pound that Pound might correct them. . . . Yeats learned tremendously
> from Pound's comments. . . . [1]

Pound's criticism has a self-confidence that convinces, or repels, by main
force. It is passionate lecturing, and impresses by its air of knowledge realized
in experience. Behind it lies the absolute conviction that the poet—especially
Pound himself—is a hero bearing the task of cultural salvation on his shoulders.
His seriousness is unmistakable; he speaks of 'our' problems. 'We appear,' he
writes in his essay on Cavalcanti (Dante's friend and fellow-poet), 'to have lost
the radiant world where one thought cuts through another with clean edge,
a world of moving energies . . . magnetisms that take form, that are seen, or
that border the visible, the matter of Dante's *Paradiso,* the glass under water,
the form that seems a form seen in a mirror.' Pound was precocious in early
defining his proper aims and in rediscovering principles of practice from his

---

1. *The Selected Letters of William Carlos Williams,* ed. John C. Thirlwall, McDowell, Obolensky,
New York, 1957, pp. 210-11. See also Yeats, *Essays,* p. 178.

studies of Romance literature, particularly of Provençal and Italian poetry. Very soon he was applying the religion of art to political and historical theory:

> Has literature a function in the state? . . . It has. . . . It has to do with the clarity and vigour of 'any and every' thought and opinion. It has to do with maintaining the very cleanliness of the tools, the health of the very matter of thought itself. . . . The individual cannot think and communicate his thought, the governor and legislator cannot act effectively or frame his laws, without words, and the solidity and validity of these words is in the care of the damned and despised *litterati*. When their work goes rotten—by that I do not mean when they express indecorous thoughts—but when their very medium, the very essence of their work, the application of word to thing goes rotten, i.e., becomes slushy or inexact, or excessive or bloated, the whole machinery of social and of individual thought and order goes to pot. This is a lesson of history. . . .[2]

But Pound's authority derives mainly from his verse. Even among the relatively imitative and 'soft' pieces of his early twenties, we shall find work of distinction. Singing lines, often brilliantly compressed, mark the early pages of *Personae: The Collected Poems*. The young poet, seeking his continuities with a British and a European past as well as with his native American one, is moving toward some new fusion of melodic, visual, and intellectual elements. These poems are both exercises and momentary culminations, such as we find in 'Ballatetta,' a graceful blending of Provençal and Romantic idealism; in the vigorously colloquial 'Cino' and 'Marvoil' and the mystical 'The Tree'; or in 'Portrait d'une Femme,' a compassionate yet satirical counterplay of matter-of-fact truths and imagined values. Ballad, sestina, *planh,* imitations of Villon and Browning—all these and similar efforts point up the poet's desire to repossess aspects of the consciousness of the past and to locate his own place in the tradition.

Then, rather suddenly, he is there. Among the poems of Pound's 1912 volume *Ripostes* we find two of the most striking lyric poems of the century, 'The Return' and 'The Alchemist.' Of the former Yeats wrote that 'it gives me better words than my own.' In this poem he saw that same baffling, shifting relationship of waking mind to dream vision which he himself was forever seeking to interpret.

'The Return,' indeed, is a superb realization of 'the radiant world where one thought cuts through another with clean edge.' The hero-gods of the ancient past, who 'exist' for us only through literature, 'return' without confidence:

> Sée they retúrn; áh sée the téntative
>
> Móvements, and the slów féet,

2. *The Literary Essays of Ezra Pound,* ed. T. S. Eliot, New Directions, New York, 1954, p. 21.

The tróuble in the pace and the uncértain

Wávering!

The 'falling' rhythmic movement here is an organic aspect of this imagined picture. The extra light syllables break up the natural gallop of the dactyl, and there is further interruption by the bunching of accented syllables in 'ah, see' and 'slow feet' and by the iambic foot with which the third line begins. These modulations give an effect of startled wonder at the very start, immediately corrected by a slowing down of the rhythm which suggests a sympathetic, pitying identification with the shades that is both muscular and psychological.

But 'they' *are* returning. The next stanza elaborates on their timidity and unsureness. However, it also accelerates the speed with which the hero-figures come into focus. Greater sharpness is gained, too, by the addition of dramatic details and vivid similes, whereas the first stanza concentrated almost entirely on generalized impressions of hesitant motion.

> See, they return, one, and by one,
> With fear, as half-awakened;
> As if the snow should hesitate
> And murmur in the wind,
>   and half turn back;
> These were the 'Wing'd-with-Awe,'
>   Inviolable.

In that last pair of lines we are swung sharply around, our attention thrust directly at the living past. Then the next stanza recovers the old sense of heroic being; in three swift, unbroken exclamations a whole world is repossessed:

> Gods of the wingèd shoe!
> With them the silver hounds,
>   sniffing the trace of air!

Finally there is the inevitable slipping away of the vision. Not at once, for the keener awareness is maintained through four more lines. But now the past tense is emphasized, and the song becomes a lament:

> Haie! Haie!
>   These were the swift to harry;
> These the keen-scented;
> These were the souls of blood.

As the poem ends, the wavering movement returns and we again see the hero-gods as they have become. The only reality left us is our awareness of the gap between vision and fact.

> Slow on the leash,
>   pallid the leash-men!

'The Alchemist' is a triumph of rhythmic 'scoring' equal, as a piece of incantation, to the dramatic conjuring of 'The Return.' This 'chant for the transmutation of metals' calls upon the female principle in all things to bring the gold to birth. It does so by invoking the names of goddesses, heroines of myth and literature, and historical personages, and with them the four elements and the realms of Paradise, Hades, and the physical universe. Images of light and burning, and of the life-force, project the alchemist's desire to see the transmutation take place. As the poem progresses, we see re-created before us the mystic unity of thought and being, imagination and sense: the world seen through medieval eyes. But the range of awareness and of reference is also the poet's own. In the self-hypnotic prayer of his alchemist we can see his own desire to 'transmute metal,' to employ in his poetry both the heritage of the whole past and his own immediate consciousness of the present, transforming them into aesthetic gold:

> Selvaggia, Guiscarda, Mandetta,
>   Rain flakes of gold on the water
> Azure and flaking silver of water,
> Alcyon, Phaetona, Alcmena,
> Pallor of silver, pale lustre of Latona,
> By these, from the malevolence of the dew
>   Guard this alembic
> Elain, Tireis, Allodetta
>   Quiet this metal.

Imagism, a much-publicized phase of the fight of Pound and others to make organic form the aim of the best poets and the expectation of their best readers, is foreshadowed and surpassed in this passage. Pound's emphasis on the single image as 'an intellectual and emotional complex in an instant of time'[3] is an aspect of his concern that the image, rather than some vague 'thought,' be recognized as the heart of poetic experience. From the pulsating centers called 'images' the poem will gain its form; rhythm, sense-effect, and structure must correspond to their guiding insight and emotion. It is characteristic of Pound that he should have taken the lead in this movement and that he should very soon have outgrown it and advanced to more complex problems.

Pound's experiments with translation added enormously to the authority of his tone and style. From the start translation afforded him the chance to sink himself into the poetry of the past and of other languages and societies. Responsive to tone and nuance, he could recover the sensibilities of others and find a voice for himself through them. His translations have the same basic virtue as his other poetry: intuitive grasp of the shape and emotional essence of his subject. Even if we do not know his originals, or are not equipped to

3. Ibid. p. 4.

read them, he convinces us that he has captured this shape and essence, has glimpsed 'the form in the air' and approximated it through the 'sculpture of rhyme.' An obvious instance is his famous rendering of the Anglo-Saxon 'Seafarer.' Here Pound cultivates a heavy, lurching, even clumsy, pounding of sound. He makes certain repetitions of consonants and phrasing that the original does not have, to stress the function of the alliteration as a major structural aspect of the Old English poem's rhythm. The effect is 'barbaric' and elemental, rhythmic as galley rowers are rhythmic; at the same time it under-scores the rigors of seafaring life. While Pound actually stays very close to a literal translation of the text, he makes it a modern poem with archaic overtones. A sailor today would not quite feel the same way as 'the seafarer' does, though he would grasp the feeling readily enough.

Even more ambitious is his work with Chinese texts, notably with the Fenellosa manuscripts. Asked to put into poetic form the scholar's prose-translations of Chinese poems in Japanese ideogram, Pound—working with Fenellosa's notes and educating himself in the process—accepted the challenge. Despite his initial ignorance of his materials and his mistakes, writes Hugh Gordon Porteus, Pound was able to grasp 'the great virtue of the Chinese language'—namely, the way in which its written characters 'contrive to suggest by their graphic gestures (as English does by its phonetic gestures) the very essence of what is to be conveyed.'[4] The ideogram itself, a stylized picture or 'graphic gesture' that has become the concrete manifestation of a sound and a concept, seemed to Pound the symbol *par excellence* of true communication, the kind that has not lost itself in abstraction. Because of it the poems of *Cathay* are by their very nature 'imagistic.'

In *Cathay* and elsewhere the word 'adaptation' may be more appropriate than 'translation.' The latter term often conceals a literal unraveling of a text which destroys what it should reveal. If the original poet were alive today, writing in *our* language and with *our* experience behind him, how would he do this poem? This is the problem Pound sets himself in his translation-adaptations.

One of Pound's major adaptations is his *Homage to Sextus Propertius* (1917). His treatment of the subtle and difficult Roman poet of the first century B.C. is based on passages from the original elegies. Pound rearranges them freely, playing on sound and association from his own standpoint as well as from that of the original text. His aim was to make an original modern poem out of the light that Propertius' sensibility and his own seemed to cast on one another. The *Homage,* he wrote, 'presents certain emotions as vital to me in 1917, faced with the infinite and ineffable imbecility of the British Empire as they were to Propertius some centuries earlier, when faced with the infinite and ineffable imbecility of the Roman Empire.'[5] He thus identifies himself with the speaker in the poem, who is 'not only Propertius but inclusive of the spirit of the young man of the Augustan Age, hating rhetoric and undeceived by imperial hog-

4. Hugh Gordon Porteus, 'Ezra Pound and His Chinese Character: A Radical Examination,' in *Ezra Pound,* ed. Peter Russell, Peter Nevill Ltd., London, 1959, p. 215.

5. *The Letters of Ezra Pound, 1907-1941,* ed. D. D. Paige, Harcourt, Brace, New York, 1950, p. 231.

wash.' Pound was thinking of the war-rhetoric of his own moment and rejoicing in the weapons the ancient poet—'tying blue ribbons in the tails of Virgil
and Horace' and 'touching words somewhat as Laforgue did'—had handed
down to him:

> Out-weariers of Apollo will, as we know, continue their
>   Martian generalities,
> We have kept our erasers in order. . . .

Pound thus uses Propertius both to attack the rhetorical sham of the Great
War and to restate certain artistic principles in a larger context than before.
It is clear not only from the *Homage* itself but from his other writings of the
time that Pound viewed the classics as rekindlers of energy rather than as inert,
soporific emblems of 'education.' 'You read Catullus,' he has observed, 'to
prevent yourself being poisoned by the lies of pundits; you read Propertius to
purge yourself of the greasy sediments of lecture courses. . . . The classics,
"ancient and modern," are precisely the acids to gnaw through the thongs and
bulls-hides with which we are tied by our schoolmasters. . . . They are almost
the only antiseptics against the contagious imbecility of mankind.'[6] The twelve
poems of the *Homage* are thus intended, not only as a faithful rendering of the
Propertian spirit but also as a counterthrust against political and academic
jargon and deception. 'There was never any question of translation, let alone
literal translation. My job was to bring a dead man to life, to present a living
figure.'[7]

That living figure, the Propertius who speaks in the *Homage*, foreshadows
the protagonist of Pound's 1919 sequence, *Hugh Selwyn Mauberley*. Like Mauberley, he speaks for the true lyric tradition as opposed to the pretentious
ponderosities of the day. He is a delicate ironist and a devotee of Aphrodite
rather than of Calliope, Muse of History. And he intermingles proud self-
assertion and self-belittling much as does Mauberley, who typifies the modern
poet. In his quick shiftings among moods and styles, too, he resembles the
speakers in *Mauberley* and in the *Cantos*. To illustrate: Poem I, which in many
ways parallels the opening 'Ode' of *Mauberley*, begins with an entranced
musical note, invoking the ghosts of the great Melic lyric tradition, then breaks
off to jeer at the 'Martian generalities' of would-be heroic poets. Next, Pound-
Propertius jauntily prophesies that he will have 'a boom after my funeral' and
that all the 'devirginated young ladies' will then love his work. But in the midst
of this buffoonery, mythical allusion is woven into the poem's fabric in the
purest evocative fashion. At last the opening poem ends on a graceful, serious
note caught up from its opening theme:

> Stands genius a deathless adornment,
>   a name not to be worn out with the years.

6. Ibid. p. 113.
7. Ibid. pp. 148-9.

In their final effect, all these shiftings make for a structural triumph revealing a complex sensibility. We must remember that Pound's adaptation is
intended not as an exercise in translation but as a new work fully expressing
Pound himself. He sets out to do deliberately what Yeats, through his 'revision'
of Arnold's 'Dover Beach' in 'A Dialogue of Self and Soul,' did unconsciously:
to bring the sensibility of the past into contemporary focus. The images by
which this sensibility unfolds itself also define an ideal poetic personality and
provide a symbolic argument made all-encompassing by the quick shiftings of
the tone. In poems VI and VII we reach the subjective center of the sequence.
These plunge into deep erotic passion, the former poem drunkenly linking the
themes of love and death (but also indulging in some wry speculation concerning the duration of Cynthia's mourning were her lover to die suddenly) and
the latter rejoicing lustily in the 'couch made happy by my long delectations'
and idealizing the mistress as a Provençal *sirventes* might. Around the passionate
center made by these two poems swirls the rest of the sequence, recapitulating
its major 'public' and aesthetic themes but also toying repeatedly with the
motifs of jealousy and fidelity. Finally, at the very end, the poet puts all worldly
cynicism aside, taking his stand' with Varro, Catullus, and all other Dionysian
poets. They are worshippers, not of Mars, but of Aphrodite—singers in the old
way of their mistresses' beauty and their own desire, 'bringing the Grecian
orgies,' as the first poem had said, 'into Italy.' And into England and America,
for that matter.

From *The Modern Poets: A Critical Introduction* (New York: Oxford Univ.
Press, 1960), pp. 49-58.

PAUL A. OLSON

Pound and the Poetry of Perception

> . . . A criticism of Pound's *Cantos* could not be better concerned . . . than in
> considering them in relation to the principal move in imaginative writing
> today—that away from the word as symbol toward the word as reality.
> —WILLIAM CARLOS WILLIAMS

IN THE introduction to the *Literary Essays of Ezra Pound,* T. S. Eliot notes a
limitation in the criticism of his senior: "He ignores Mallarmé; he is uninterest-
ed in Baudelaire." The objection is that Pound is unappreciative of the major
symboliste poets. The passage may, I think, be a touchstone to two strains in
modern writing. Eliot, Pound, Joyce, and Lewis are frequently lumped together
in a common mash, given identical political opinions and identical literary
techniques. Pound is supposed to have made forms into which Eliot and other
friends of his dumped thought. Such boxes have a vague neatness; they permit
one to ignore both form and content or, what is more important, they permit
one to ignore the extent to which the form of a poem arises from the urgencies
of its content. Eliot's later poetry has a thing to say and a way of saying it,
as does also Pound's. Eliot's master in France is Baudelaire, and he has reason
to wish him praised. Pound, on the other hand, looks more to Gautier, has
learned little from either Mallarmé or Baudelaire. Moreover, Eliot is a symbolist while Pound is not, in any of the usual senses of the term. Herein lies a
difference in method which associates Pound with Gautier and separates him
not only from Eliot but from a whole school of modern writers who stem out
of Poe and his French followers: Yeats, Joyce, Thomas, Crane.

The distinction which I am attempting to define is not a slight one; it affects
Pound's conception of the epistemological basis of poetry, its important traditions, and its ultimate purpose. It may, perhaps, be defined by the phrases "the
poetry of perception" and "the poetry of vision." The poetry of perception,
Pound's kind of verse, deals with the seen world, the act of perception, the finer
sensations. The poetry of vision, Eliot's kind, if it is interested in the seen thing
at all, is interested in it only as it intimates some meaning beyond itself. Here,
to adopt the jargon of contemporary criticism, the *logos* speaks through the flesh
of experience. Symbolist poetry commonly incarnates vision: death's other
kingdom, Mrs. Yeats's nocturnal phantasies, H. C. Earwicker's waking sleep.
Knowledge of such arcana could come from no ordinary experience if it may
be said to come from experience at all; it is a kind of revelation before which
the dizziness of experience is stilled.

In getting at the attitudes underlying these two kinds of poetry, Baudelaire and Gautier may help. Gautier said, "Je suis un homme pour qui le monde extérieur existe." Baudelaire wrote:

> La nature est un temple où de vivants piliers
> Laissent parfois sortir de confuses paroles;
> L'homme y passe à travers des fôrets de symboles,
> Qui l'observent avec des regards familiers.

Gautier's world exists, solid, there to be probed with microscopic eye. Because of his belief in a "solid" world, Chiari rightly places the French poet not only with the Parnassans but with such naturalistic performers as Zola and Courbet. Baudelaire's world speaks. This is, I suppose, the justification for his use of symbolist techniques. The words in his poetry have a meaning beyond themselves because the objects to which they point—specifically, in the walking through the forest—articulate a meaning beyond themselves. It is probable that symbolism worthy of the name always implies some kind of surrender to modes of looking at the world not dependent on collection of empirical data.

The business of attitudes toward the sources of truth in poetry is crucial. I would suggest that the difference between Gautier and Baudelaire, between Pound and let us say Eliot, turns on a differing response to the study of physical phenomena, to the rise of science. Dante and Spenser, the English romantics and French *symbolistes* all share part of that common heritage with regard to the nature of poetic perception which says that eternity may be seen in a forest, on a trip through the Alps, or in a grain of sand. Dante and Spenser wrote before the sacramental conception of the universe had been questioned by science. Little feeling of conscious rebellion against the appearances obtrudes into their poetry. Baudelaire and his successors turned to a somewhat similar view of things specifically to get away from pragmatism and naturalism, the jail of experience which physical studies had built for nineteenth-century man. The method of Pound and Gautier is an alternative way, perhaps the only alternative way, of preserving the claims of poetry in an age of science. That way substitutes a form of cooperation with science for its rejection. Instead of denying the world of the microscope while seeking a kingdom beyond it, the poet collaborates though reserving his special "poetical" claims.

For Pound, the choice between the poetry of vision and the poetry of perception was a deliberate thing. He deliberately chose the latter. Pound has tirelessly asserted that the method of science is also the method of good poetry, most clearly in his *ars poetica,* Fenellosa's essay on the Chinese written character, but also in his *ABC of Reading* and his criticism of individual authors. Poetry, like science, deals in the direct treatment of the thing. Both watch the transfer of force between things.

Poetry retains its special values. While the method of science requires the transformation of observation into mathematical symbols or technical vocabulary, the maker of verses resents the loss of raw experience implied in such transformations. He keeps his world whole. Chinese poetry, the highest order 'of verse according to Pound's canons, allows the seen thing to remain a picture in thought. Pound objects to the modern scientist who does not see the forces with which he deals, "the rose that his magnet makes in the steel filings." Not accidentally, among the heroes in the *Cantos* are to be found the scientists, the Curie's, Frobenius, Remy de Gourmont (between science and poetry), and the gentlemen at the mathematical congress "mit tearsz hrolling tdown dhere vaces" (*Canto* 87). Seeing is everything with Pound:

> watch the time like a hawk . . .
> ½ research and   ½ techne
> ½ observation,   ½ techne
> ½ training,   ½ techne
>   (*Canto* 85)

While the *Cantos* include what might be taken for visions (d'Este remembering Roland), these do not involve unusual sources of knowledge. They are heightened perceptions, the record of what has been or might be imagined by various historical personages. Or they are part of the satiric machinery of the poem; Hell in *Canto* XIV has about the same usefulness for Pound which Rosicrucian theology has for Pope. In a significant essay on W. H. Hudson entitled *Hudson: Poet Strayed into Science,* Pound expends a good deal of praise on Hudson's fusion of the roles of naturalist and literary man. He also defines there his attitude toward seeing, toward whatever vision he accepts. "As long as Christendom is permeated with the superstition that the human body is tainted and that the senses are not noble avenues of 'illumination,' where is the basis of a glory in the color sense without which bird wings are unapprehended . . . ?" The poet on the side of science joys in the very act of perceiving, in the splendor of the seen world; there is little other illumination in the *Cantos.*

To Pound, the symbolists who sought another kind of insight indulged a muzzyheadedness akin to wishful thinking. He speaks of "the funny symboliste trappings, 'sin,' 'satanism,' rosy cross, heavy lilies, Jersey Lilies, etc.,

> 'Ch'hanno perduto il ben dell'intelletto.' "

In losing the good of the rational intellect, the symbolists "degraded the symbol to the status of a word":

> They made it a form of metonomy. One can be grossly "symbolic," for example, by using the term "cross" to mean "trial." The symbolist's *symbols* have a fixed value, like numbers in arithmetic, like 1, 2, and 7.

That is, the symbolist's counters had no reality behind them, either transcendental or immanent; consequently, they became simply an elaborate species of circumlocution. Pound recognizes the ancestry of the nineteenth-century *symbolistes* in the medieval allegorists, but he is no more happy about medieval allegory. He resists Valli's attempts to "simbologize" Cavalcanti and criticizes

Dante's unfortunate terminology when referring to the three typological levels of the *Commedia*. What Pound finds in his beloved Dante, I suspect, is chiefly precise observation; what he praises in Cavalcanti is his dependence on the medieval "empirical" philosophers: Albertus ("for the proof by experience"), Roger Bacon, the Arabic Aristotelians. His own long poem about history is, like Cavalcanti's *Donna,* a work founded on "natural dimostramento."

From "Pound and the Poetry of Perception," *Thought,* 35 (1960), 331-48.

ROY HARVEY PEARCE

Ezra Pound's Epic

HALFWAY THROUGH Canto 85, in the midst of a passage of broken musings on the failure of the "understanding" in the nineteenth century, appear these sharply cadenced lines:

> No classics,
>   no American history,
>   no centre, no general root,
> No *prezzo giusto* as core.

The *Cantos* are an attempt to remedy this radical defect. ("UBI JUS VAGUM," Pound writes in the line following the four quoted.) They supply, however, not a single center but a series—a constellation of exemplars of *prezzo giusto* and its contraries by means of which the center and the reader who will seek it may be defined. The *Cantos* consist of a complex of centers, the perception of which is ordered by the absolutely decorous management of "degrees and weights of importance." (I speak here as much of what the *Cantos* are intended to do as what they *do* do. No one, so far as I know, has yet reported on a mastery of them adequate enough to guarantee his interpretation of their substance and their theory.) In effect, they evoke not a single sensibility (writer-reader) which will make itself one with its world, but rather a group of sensibilities which will be the means whereby one sensibility (the writer) will teach another sensibility (the reader) how it may relate itself to its world and so know and control its destiny. What should emerge from the *Cantos* is a sense of propadeutic control; the assemblage of centers that is the poem is, for Pound, the only proper Paideuma. It constitutes a rediscovery, a making new, of what are for Pound the noblest, truest, and surest elements in culture, a rediscovery so powerful in its stylistic precision that it will irresistibly reconstitute the sensibility, and thus the political morality,[1] of him who would give himself over

---

1. The relation between art and political-economic morality is made explicit in the well-known passage from Canto 45:

> with usura the line [of the painter] grows thick
> with usura is no clear demarcation
> and no man can find site for his dwelling.
> Stone cutter is kept from his stone
> weaver is kept from his loom

The idea is developed in many other places, notably: *Guide to Kulchur* (London, 1938), p. 27; *Carta da Visita* (Rome, 1942), as discussed by Davenport, "Pound and Frobenius"; letter to Carlo Izzo,

to reading it—someone akin to the "cosmic man" whom Wyndham Lewis envisaged for America at the end of the forties.[2] It is a brief but all-comprehending encyclopedia which walks and talks like a man. "There is no mystery about the Cantos," Pound wrote in his *Guide to Kulchur*, " . . . they are the tale of the tribe—give Rudyard credit for his use of the phrase. No one has claimed that the Malatesta Cantos are obscure. They are openly volitionist, establishing, I think clearly, the effect of the factive [this would appear to be Pound's neologism for "fictive" and "factitive"] personality, Sigismundo, an entire man." In Pound's hands, the new tale of the tribe, the new epic, becomes openly volitionist and entirely factive—willing and making, through its collocation of centers (Sigismundo Malatesta, his corruption glossed over, is one such), a new Paideuma for a new world.

Defining even the gross structure of the *Cantos* is as difficult as defining the gross structure of *Song of Myself,* and for analogous reasons. This also is a poem which contrives rather than memorializes its hero—or rather, its series of heroes. They are persons whose sheer volitional and factive existence, decorously communicated, serves to create an ideal type, one who is out there, just beyond the confines of the latest *Canto:* believed in, aspired toward, sought after, perhaps to be imitated. There is no plot. There is no necessary beginning or end, except as Pound's perceptions make them necessary. Process is as central a concept for him as it was for Whitman: as it has to be in an epic which would make rather than commemorate. The process must be kept going, for the centers of reality which it would constellate are themselves in process. The core is a living core, to be understood in terms of effect, not of cause. Hence, it seems proper for Pound to say that Canto 100 will likely not be the end and that one cannot yet conceive of the "total organism."[3] We have been given various attempts at assessing the total organism, from Yeats's celebrated account of the *Cantos* as fugue, through the emphasis on metamorphosis in Pound's letter to his father in 1927, to Pound's Dantesque statement to an exegete in 1953: "My *Paradiso* will have no St Dominic or Augustine, but it will be a *Paradiso* just the same, moving toward final coherence. I'm getting at the building of the City, that whole tradition."[4] In any case, we cannot be sure; and we might well extend the applications of some words from a 1939 letter of Pound: "God damn Yeats' bloody paragraph. Done more to prevent people reading Cantos for what is *on the page* than any other one smoke screen." In the same letter Pound concluded: "As to the *form* of the *Cantos:* All I can say or pray is: *wait* till it's

---

8 January 1938, *Letters,* p. 303.

2. In *America and Cosmic Man* (London, 1948).

3. This is reported (from an interview with Pound, 20 July 1953) by Davenport, "Pound and Frobenius," pp. 32 and 52.

4. William Butler Yeats, *A Vision* (New York, 1956), pp. 4-5; letter to H. L. Pound, 11 April 1927, *Letters,* p. 210; Davenport, "Pound and Frobenius," p. 52. Cf. a statement of Pound's quoted, undated, by N. H. Pearson in his Preface to John Edwards, *Preliminary Checklist of the Writings of Ezra Pound* (New Haven, 1953), p. viii: "For forty years I have schooled myself . . . to write an epic poem which begins 'In the Dark Forest,' crosses the Purgatory of human error, and ends in the light, 'fra i maestri di color che sanno.' "

there. I mean wait till I get 'em written and then if it don't show, I will start exegesis. I haven't an Aquinas-map; Aquinas *not* valid now."[5]

Such exegesis as we can start—and likely such as we will conclude with—centers on the "ideogrammic method." In the history of Pound's career, movement toward the theory of the ideogram, as is well known, has proceeded thus: image > vortex > ideogram. That he successively refined his theory of the image and its functioning until he arrived at a stage where he felt that language itself could be made to work non-discursively (or, as we have been recently urged to say, presentationally); that the crucial catalyst in this segment of the history of his thought is his discovery of the possibilities of Chinese as a language which still worked, to a significant measure, pre- (or infra-) discursively; that although his theories are wrong according to even the most charitable of sinologists, they nonetheless are right for the kind of poem he aspires toward—all these facts are by now well enough known and need only to be recalled here. They have recently been ordered, put in their proper setting, and analyzed and evaluated thus:

> . . . the 'dissociation of sensibility' . . . is an attempt to project upon the history of poetry a modern theory of the image. This theory owes something to Blake, and something to Coleridge; through the French symbolists it owes something to Schopenhauer, and through Hulme something to Bergson. Before Mr. Eliot made his particular projection of it, it was familiar to Yeats (who got it directly from Blake and indirectly through Symons) and to Pound, who got it from Symons and de Gourmont and the French poets themselves. Ultimately this is the product of over a century of continuous anti-positivist poetic speculation, defining and defending the poet's distinct and special way of knowing truth. It involves a theory of form which excludes or strictly subordinates all intellectual speculation, and which finds in music, and better still in the dance, an idea of what art should be: entirely free of discursive content, thinking in quite a different way from the scientists. . . . Form and meaning are co-essential, and the image belongs not to the mechanical world of intellect, but to the vital world of intuition; it is the aesthetic monad of the Symbolists, the Image of the Imagists, the Vortex of the Vorticists, and finally the ideogram of Pound.[6]

This is by now an authoritative statement. But one element needs to be added properly to bring Pound's theory of the ideogram into the purview here set for us and at the same time to move it one step out of that purview, into the world of the new Paideuma. "Knowing truth" must be changed to something like "using truth and putting it into action," making it factive and volitional.

5. To Hubert Creekmore, February 1939, *Letters*, pp. 321, 323.
6. Frank Kermode, "Dissociation of Sensibility," *Kenyon Review*, XIX (1957), pp. 180-181. Mr. Kermode puts these matters into their largest context in his brilliant *Romantic Image* (London, 1957).

Pound has, of course, been quite explicit about his ideogrammic method. He wrote in *Guide to Kulchur:*

> The ideogramic [sic] method consists in presenting one facet and then another until at some point one gets off the dead and desensitized surface of the reader's mind, onto a part that will register.
>
> "The 'new' angle being new to the reader who cannot always be the same reader. The newness of the angle being relative and the writer's aim, at least this writer's aim [,] being revelation, a just revelation irrespective of newness or oldness.

Such considerations as these led him to say, a little later in the *Guide:* "The history of a culture is the history of ideas going into action." Ideas, that is to say, as ideograms; for such ideas *are* culture and work on men to cultivate them. " 'The character of the man is revealed in every brushstroke' (and this does not apply only to the [Chinese] ideogram)." The *Cantos,* then, working ideogrammically, with a totally decorous attendance to "degrees and weights of importance," reveal character, and revealing it, would make it new and so teach the new Paideuma.

The pedagogical task implied here is outlined quite straightforwardly in a section of Pound's translation of the Confucian *Great Digest* (the brackets in the quotation are Pound's):

> 4. The men of old wanting to clarify and diffuse throughout the empire that light which comes from looking straight into the heart and then acting, first set up good government in their own states; wanting good government in their states, they first established order in their own families; wanting order in the home, they first disciplined themselves; desiring self-discipline, they rectified their own hearts; and wanting to rectify their hearts, they sought precise verbal definitions of their inarticulate thoughts [the tones given off by the heart]; wishing to attain precise verbal definitions, they set to extend their knowledge to the utmost. This completion of knowledge is rooted in sorting things into organic categories.
>
> 5. When things had been classified in organic categories, knowledge moved toward fulfillment; given the extreme knowable points, the inarticulate thoughts were defined with precision, [the sun's lance coming to rest in the precise spot verbally]. Having attained this precise verbal definition [*aliter,* this sincerity], they then stabilized their hearts, they disciplined themselves; having attained self-discipline, they set their own houses in order; having order in their own homes, they brought good government to their own states: and when their states were well governed, the empire was brought into equilibrium.
>
> 6. From the Emperor, Son of Heaven, down to the common man singly and all together, this self-discipline is the root.
>
> 7. If the root be in confusion, nothing will be well governed.

In the end-product of some such process as this lies Pound's hopes for the *Cantos*, which are his hopes for his world. (The statement quoted is in fact paraphrased in Canto 13.) But he must also bring to bear in this process forces deriving from a plenitude of history far beyond that taken into account in the Confucian Paideuma. "An epic," he wrote Harriet Monroe in 1933, "includes history and history ain't all slush and babies' pink toes."[7] He would, in short, lay bare the roots of heroic character through a rendering of universal history.

The character is that of a group of Pound's own heroes who have in common the fact that they went adventuring (in time and space, or in mind, or in both) and sought, in the step-by-step manner described in the Confucian passage quoted above, to bring their empires into equilibrium. All were bearers of the sun's lance. What they did and what they said—these are for Pound ideas in action. He would represent his heroes—Odysseus, Sigismundo Malatesta, Jefferson, Adams, Frobenius, Apollonius of Tyana, rulers out of the great periods of Chinese history, many artists—in such a way that their deeds and sayings are not values but modes of valuation. We are to be brought face to face with those deeds and sayings, are not to be allowed to have such perspective in them as will let us use them as mere counters. Biographical details, quotations from an ever-widing range of authorities, intruded estimations, translations, imitations, ideograms, and pictograms, and all the other *disjecta membra* set down in the *Cantos* —these are rendered and arranged so that we will soon give up hoping to put them back into their context in historical actuality; willy-nilly, we are to grant the poet's claim that in such contexts their meanings have come to be hopelessly tangled and confused. Our comprehension of them is to be controlled by the juxtapositions the poet makes and by the possibilities for metered progression which he discovers. We are to know them for what they *do*. They are propadeutic to our struggle to define ourselves anew.

History, in the broadest and most inclusive sense, becomes for the poet the only authentic language. But even that language has become corrupt; and the poet's obligation is to cleanse it by tearing it—but with loving care—out of its matrix in sheer factuality and by getting to the roots of its moments of truth. For him facts are true to the degree that, as we know them, they lead us to classify things in organic categories, so to attain in turn verbal precision, self-discipline, and social and political equilibrium. Such a criterion for truth not only directs Pound's choice of materials for the *Cantos* but his way of presenting them. Indeed, they appear to present themselves; a reader's only clue to their relevance in given places in the poem is his sudden, startled awareness that he is interested in them not for their value as "fact" but for the value as "truth"—truth as the poet would bid him conceive of it. Facts which are in this sense true are "ideas in action"—Pound's definition of history. Thus the concept of the "factive." It directs Pound to take into account only so much of his protagonists' deeds as will comport with his criterion for truth—not an actual Sigismundo Malatesta but a "true" one, not an actual Adams but a "true" one, not an actual Jew but a "true" one, perhaps not even an actual Pound but

7. 14 September 1933, *Letters*, ed. Paige, p. 247.

a "true" one. History, then, is not given to Pound; he takes it, and exclusively on his own terms. Either we accept the terms or decide that Pound has betrayed history, all the while claiming that it has betrayed him. In the *Cantos,* in either case, his is the last word. Its devices and techniques, however, are intended to be means of proving that the first word was history's and that the poet has only been echoing it in such a way as to recover it in its pristine state. Pound's mood is that of the Confucius who says in Canto 13, " ' . . . even I can remember / A day when the historians left blanks in their writings, / But that time seems to be passing.' " The burden on the reader, if he would be drawn into the vortices of the *Cantos,* is not to abandon all hope as he enters there.[8]

In the first seventy-one *Cantos,* ideograms (which lead to centers and cores of *prezzo giusto* and its contraries) are developed in rich and proliferating detail. Historical emphasis is on the achievements of Malatesta, and of early national American culture and Chinese culture—all counterpointed against the initial narrative of Odysseus' voyage. Again and again the matter of usury, with its alienating effect, turns up. Language shifts suddenly, even to Chinese ideograms themselves; historical records are quoted directly or are paraphrased; movement is freely back and forward in time. The total effect is vertiginously clear. One is often at a loss to relate one item to another, yet he is (whenever he can supply himself with the right learning and information) crystal-clear as to the specific quality of each item. (Pound himself furnishes a useful gloss to him who first looks into the *Cantos:* "Very well, I am not proceeding according to Aristotelian logic but according to the ideogramic method of first heaping together the necessary components of thought."[9] The movement of the poem is even more accelerated in Cantos 74 and following (72 and 73 have not been published). The *Pisan* section (74-84) centers on Pound himself as he pulls out of the world he has created material whereby he may comprehend his own

8. The reader of the *Cantos* must be particularly indebted to such exegetical studies as these: Hugh Kenner, *The Poetry of Ezra Pound* (London, 1951); Harold Watts, *Ezra Pound and The Cantos* (London, 1951); the essayists in *Motive and Method in The Cantos of Ezra Pound* and in *Ezra Pound,* ed. P. Russell (London, 1950); Clark Emory, *Ideas into Action* (Miami, 1958); two unpublished dissertations—E. M. Glenn, *Association and The Cantos of Ezra Pound* (Stanford, 1955) and Angela Jung, *Ezra Pound and China* (Washington, 1956); and two serial publications devoted mainly to Pound—*The Pound Newsletter* (University of California, Berkeley, 1954-1956) and *The Analyst* (Northwestern University, 1953-   ). One can only say, with Whitman, "Hurrah for positive science!"

Pound wrote in his 1939 letter to Creekmore, from which I have already quoted, p. 94: "I believe that when finished, *all* foreign words in the Cantos, Gk., etc. will be underlinings, not necessary to the sense, in any way. I mean a complete sense will exist without them; it will be there in the American text, but the Greek, [Chinese] ideograms, etc., will indicate a *duration* from whence or since when." This is again the theory of "weights and measures"—as though Pound would manage the English we certainly know in such a way as to make it define words (and ideograms) in languages of which we have no knowledge whatsoever; so that in turn we will know what these words mean and thereby sense their durative value: which I take to mean the power they have of establishing concretely and particularly the exact provenience and resonance of meanings which they have in the cultures whose words they properly are. Pound would teach us foreign languages primarily in terms of contexts, not of semantic content. We would need no informants, only Pound's printed page. Even his most enthusiastic exegetes have boggled at this.

9. *The ABC of Economics* [1933] (London, 1953), p. 27.

destiny, and through his that of modern man. These are, in the perhaps
Dantesque scheme of the poem, the purgatorial Cantos; it is here that Pound
breaks through to the great statements he has (according to the scheme of the
poem) earned the right to make—the passages that begin "nothing matters but
the quality / of the affection—" (76) and the one that begins "The ant's a /
centaur in his dragon world" (81).

The Pisan Cantos stabilize the whole, in preparation for the series of almost
Mosaic pronouncements of the *Rock-Drill Cantos* (85-95). Here, as the working
title indicates, Pound would drill holes for explosives, so as to move mountains
and collect that part of them worth making new. These *Cantos* move with a
rush of new insight; the ideogrammic mode achieves its fullest and richest and
most literal use. Drawing from such widely disparate sources as the *Chou King*,
a classic of Chinese history, from Thomas Hart Benton's *Thirty Years View*,
and Philostratus' account of Apollonius of Tyana, marked by less of the
extended personal, lyrical passages than is the Pisan group, these *Cantos* (so far
as one can work his way into them) carry a sense of certitude and assurance
that is at once apocalyptic and sublime. Their most important hero is Apollonius and a series of equivalents for him—all beneficent magician-creators, as
Pound himself would now be.

Now at the edge of what he has called his paradise, in Canto 92, the poet
looks back:

> And against usury
>   and the degradation of sacraments,
> For 40 years I have seen this,
>   now flood as the Yang tse
> also desensitization
>   25 hundred years desensitization
>   a thousand years, desensitization
> After Apollonius, desensitization
>   & a little light from the borders:
>   Erigena,
>   Avicenna, Richardus

He had first glimpsed manifestations of that little light in the heroes of the
earlier Cantos. Now he seeks heroes to whom the light not only gives charis-
matic authority but those who have had direct access to it. His paradise is yet
to come; he would see the light too. Canto 90 ends: "UBI AMOR IBI
OCULUS EST." The question shifts from: How make it new? to: In what light
make it new? For what one sees in the light of this truth one truly loves:

> Trees die & the dream remains
>   Not love but that love flows from it
>   ex animo
>   & cannot ergo delight in itself

but only in the love flowing from it.
UBI AMOR IBI OCULUS EST.

Where love is, the poet would be. If history is ideas in action, the act is one of love—by which the poet and his protagonists, out of some sublime necessity, have been created. The distortions and perversions of historical fact and the violence and hatred which so often emerge in the *Cantos* —these demonstrate at the very least that the light can be blinding. Stumbling over the villainy of some of his heroes, Pound can yet pretend that it has never existed—or at least, has existed to a good end—because he cannot quite see it for what to the uninitiated it really seems to be. Sensing that there are men and events just beyond his field of vision, he can curse them for not being within it:

> *Democracies electing their sewage*
> *till there is no clear thought about holiness*
> *a dung flow from 1913*
> *and, in this, their kikery functioned, Marx, Freud*
> *and the american beaneries,*
> *   Maritain, Hutchins,*
> *or as Benda remarked: "La trahison"*   (91)

The question of who betrayed whom nonetheless remains an open one. Perhaps Pound's achievement is to have forced it. Perhaps he will turn out to have been the Ossian of the twentieth century. The important point for the history of American aspirations toward an epic, for Pound's search for a new Paideuma in which substance and the means to comprehend substance would be identical, is that betrayal has been a necessary condition for discovery of truth, hatred a necessary condition for love. As Whitman's love for himself would drive him to transforming all other selves into aspects of himself in order that he might love them, so Pound's love for himself would drive him to destroy all other selves whose existence his idea of love will prevent him from loving. Whitman's and Pound's means to making an American epic are thus diametrically opposed, but they have at least this in common: they ask that their poetry lead to a totally unifying sacramentalism. To know, is for Whitman, to become; for Pound, to become or be destroyed. Such propositions surely are urged or assented to in vain. But the fact is that they have been urged, assented to, and acted upon. In the process, Barlow's dream of winning a true passage to the heart of youth, of making the poem the means of creating an infinitude of American heroes, turns out to have been not entirely visionary; but, like most visions, it has always had its component of nightmare. Seeing what assenting to the vision has demanded of him, the American should not too much regret his lost youth. Yet the vision is such stuff as his life has been made on.

From *The Continuity of American Poetry* (Princeton: Princeton Univ. Press, 1961), pp. 91-101.

GEORGE DEKKER

Poetic Motive and Strategy in the *Cantos*

THE BEST point of entry to *The Cantos* is without a doubt the first canto. A reader coming to the poem for the first time will make little sense out of later cantos unless he has mastered the earlier sections. However, for the purposes of this study, Canto XIII is the best point of departure: the implications of this canto must be grasped if we are to understand the rest of the poem, and especially if we are to understand the so-called 'Hell Cantos', numbers XIV and XV. For that vigorous attack on contemporary society, disparaged by Mr Eliot and celebrated by Miss Sitwell,[1] forms a jarring antithesis to the contemplative ease of

> Kung walked
>> by the dynastic temple
> and into the cedar grove,
>> and then out by the lower river,
> And with him Khieu Tchi
>> and Tian the low speaking

But XIII is not a 'lyrical' canto:

> And 'we are unknown,' said Kung,
> 'You will take up charioteering?
>> 'Then you will become known,
> 'Or perhaps I should take up charioteering, or archery?
> 'Or the practice of public speaking?'

The noteworthy point is that Kung (Confucius) suddenly turns the question on himself. (I) We know well enough that he ought to do just what he is doing: perambulating and questioning, after the fashion of all sages. But this act of self-interrogation illustrates his own doctrine, which is shortly revealed. After each of his disciples has described his personal ambition ('What would you do to become known?')

> . . . Kung smiled upon all of them equally.

---

1. Eliot, *After Strange Gods* (New York, 1934), pp. 45-7; Edith Sitwell, *Aspects of Modern Poetry* (1934), pp. 178-214.

> And Thseng-sie desired to know:
>   'Which had answered correctly?'
> And Kung said, 'They have all answered correctly,
>   'That is to say, each in his nature.'

It is clear that Canto XIII begins as a sort of treatise on education. The first step, apparently, is for the teacher to question his own fitness for the job: '*Or perhaps I should* take up charioteering, or archery?' The second step is to determine the student's individual aptitudes: 'They have all answered correctly,/ That is to say, each in his own nature.' And the third step is to insist on the development of their talent:

> And Kung raised his cane against Yuan Jang,
> Yuan Jang being his elder,
> For Yuan Jang sat by the roadside pretending to
>   be receiving wisdom.
> And Kung said
>   'You old fool, come out of it,
> 'Get up and do something useful.'
>   And Kung said
> 'Respect a child's faculties
> 'From the moment it inhales the clear air,
> 'But a man of fifty who knows nothing
>   'Is worthy of no respect.'

The final step is for the state to put developed talents to use:

> And 'When the prince has gathered about him
> 'All the savants and artists, his riches will be
>   fully employed.'

When the treatise on education reaches the level of the prince, it changes, by the most natural transition, into a treatise on government:

> And Kung said, and wrote on the bo leaves:
>   'If a man have not order within him
> 'He can not spread order about him;
> 'And if a man have not order within him
> 'His family will not act with due order;
>   'And if the prince have not order within him
> 'He can not put order in his dominions.'

At first glance, this passage may seem rather repetitious, and as a matter of fact the typographical layout rather hinders than helps perception. Grammatically, the last six lines consist of three almost exactly parallel sentences. The purpose of this somewhat uncomfortable construction is to mimic the sense, which is that Everyman, prince and peasant *alike,* observes the same rule of self-government. The discomfort one experiences when reading this passage arises from one's feeling that the second and third lines state a principle that governs the fourth and fifth lines (one unit) and the sixth and seventh lines (a second unit), and that, therefore, the last four lines should be clearly subordinate to the two preceding lines. But by making the sentences parallel, Pound seeks to undermine the habit of thinking in hierarchical terms.[2]

So much for political and grammatical theory. But the treatise on government is not finished yet. Theory, if it is to be useful, is the product of careful observation within a reasonably limited field; and so, in the next few lines, we find that Kung's working vocabulary reflects a preoccupation with what is close to the world where one touches and is touched.

> And Kung gave the words 'order'
> and 'brotherly deference'
> And said nothing of the 'life after death'.
> And he said
>   'Anyone can run to excesses,
> 'It is easy to shoot past the mark,
> 'It is hard to stand firm in the middle.'
>
> And they said: 'If a man commit murder
>   'Should his father protect him, and hide him?'
> And Kung said:
>   'He should hide him.'

There may be some argument as to the rightness of Kung's answer, but the distinction he makes is a humane one: to hide the son is one's duty; and this is not anti-social, because kinship is the primary social component. (Whether to *protect* the son is a separate issue, which involves the father in joining his son against society.)

Thus the study of government moves from theory to practical counsel; and, as one expects from a teacher who starts by questioning his own fitness to teach, it moves from practical counsel to personal practice:

> And Kung gave his daughter to Kong-Tchang
>   Although Kong-Tchang was in prison.
> And he gave his niece to Nan-Young
>   although Nan-Young was out of office.

Having brought order within himself, Kung's decisions are not influenced by fear of public opinion. It is clear that, though I speak of moving from theory to practical counsel to personal practice, there has been no movement: gov-

2. My 'Everyman' is unfortunate, since it implies a hierarchy in which the spiritual being is distinct from and higher than the worldly being; Pound is interested in 'man' rather than 'Man'.

ernment begins and ends with, 'If a man have not order within him / He can not spread order about him'. Kung acts, counsels, and theorizes wisely because, to begin with, he has order within him.

The third part of Canto XIII contains a sort of treatise on good professional practice. Since governing is the profession which affects everybody, the prince is treated first:

> And Kung said, 'Wan ruled with moderation.
>   'In his day the State was well kept,
> 'And even I can remember
> 'A day when the historians left blanks in their writings,
> 'I mean for things they didn't know,
> 'But that time seems to be passing.'
> And Kung said, 'Without character you will
>   be unable to play on that instrument
> 'Or to execute the music fit for the Odes.

'Character' is the key word here, just as 'nature' and 'order' were the key words in earlier sections of this canto. The word 'character' as Pound uses it here implies more than moral strength, it seems to imply a firmness of outline, a clearly delimited identity—as well it might, since its Latin stem denoted a branding mark, and its Old French ancestor *charassein* denoted 'to sharpen, to engrave'. (There are far less remote usages which correspond to Pound's, but the backgrounds may serve to bring his usage into relief.) It is apparent that this definition is in line with Kung's concern to distinguish individual aptitudes and to govern oneself so far as not to be swayed by a fear of public opinion.

It is, presumably, 'character' which caused Wang to rule 'with moderation' (from *moderor:* to set bounds to, to check, to moderate, to restrain). To rule with moderation means, apparently, not to rule too much, not to impose the royal will too heavily. Likewise, the historian who has 'character' does not try to impose his will on his materials; without integrity of his own, he will fail to respect (or even recognize) the integrity of his materials. The player who has 'character', like the good historian, does not 'project': the Odes exist independent of himself, and it is his business to 'execute' the music for them, not to 'interpret'. The man who makes history, the man who records it, and the man who makes music for the eternal Odes—each must honour the integrity of his 'subject'; he must neither meddle with nor fake an understanding of it. Just as the teacher must be sure of his own vocation before he prepares others for a vocation, and as a man must have order within him before he can spread order about him, so must a man have character before he can do his job without tyrannizing his subject.

The admirable precepts which Canto XIII offers might, of course, be reduced to 'know thyself'; but the reduction merely obfuscates what I may have already obfuscated by too much commentary. Indeed, the last passage discussed might serve as a text for Pound's poetic practice in *The Cantos*. In some respects Pound was of all men the least prepared to follow the teachings of Confucius, so that, all too frequently, one recalls Canto XIII as a monument of self-deception; yet *The Cantos* would not be what it is if Pound had not taken Confucius seriously. The so-called 'Hell Cantos', which I have described as an antithesis to Canto XIII, furnish a striking example of poetry which can be best understood by the application of Pound's Confucian precepts, and which can be judged quite severely enough without recourse to other standards.

> 'The blossoms of the apricot
>   blow from the east to the west,
> 'And I have tried to keep them from falling.'

From *Sailing After Knowledge: The Cantos of Ezra Pound* (London: Routledge & Kegan Paul, 1963), pp. 3-7.

NOEL STOCK

Pound's Style and Method

THE BEST and bulk of Pound's literary prose was written before 1920. Whatever shortcomings it may have, it was written by one who was interested not only in what he was writing about, but the literary world in which he was working as well. The later prose, even the best of it, even essays like 'How to read', 'Date Line' and those on Monro and Housman, lack the freshness of the earlier pieces, despite the chatty and occasionally effective style; but more than that, they are the work of a man who for critical purposes has lost touch with the literature he is discussing and the literary world for which he is writing, and is engaged in the arbitrary arrangement of categories and often disembodied guesses. Despite the tone of succinct wisdom with which these categories and guesses are laid out and related—related, that is to say, in the sense that Pound puts them together—there are no filaments of thought binding them into a whole. Relationships, all sorts of strange relationships, are thrust upon them by Pound's short sharp prose, which has a habit of outrunning both Pound and reality and creating a sealed-off world of its own. . . .

At what point we should begin to blame Ernest Fenollosa for Pound's later prose and method is hard to say, for although he wrote about Fenollosa and the 'ideogramic' method on a number of occasions, he did not explain what he meant by it. Or rather, he wrote three or four explanations which look simple enough at first sight, but are not always easy to interpret when one comes to consider them in detail. Fenollosa, if he did not actually cause Pound's style and method, seems at any rate to have confirmed him in the employment of certain ideas which led in this direction. As I pointed out in my discussion of Fenollosa's influence on the poems of the *Lustra* period, Fenollosa's widow gave Pound her husband's papers in 1913. Among them was a long essay called 'The Chinese Written Character as a Medium for Poetry', which, according to Pound, was 'practically finished' by its author. 'I have done little more', he wrote in 1918, 'than remove a few repetitions and shape a few sentences.' Pound published the essay first in serial form in the *Little Review* during 1919, in his own prose book *Instigations* (1920), and later as a separate booklet in 1936.

Beyond any doubt it enables us to look again with a fresh eye at certain aspects of the language of poetry. Whatever questionable things he may have said, about Shakespeare rarely using the word 'is', for instance, he does occasionally stir our reason and imagination by virtue of his insight into the relation between the language of poetry and the energies and forces which pulse, dart, flow, uncoil and merge in the world about us. He does not define this relation carefully, for he is intent mainly on the physical world as something mechanical, and also on proving a theory; but there are precious insights—old problems perceived from a new angle—for anyone who is willing to look for them. With all that he says or suggests about images and freshness of language, it is not hard to see why he appealed to the Pound of the *Lustra* period, and his influence at this stage was all to the good, confirming Pound in what he had been aiming at for several years before he saw the Fenollosa papers, and at the same time acting as a stimulant, and introducing Pound to the world of Chinese poetry.

Our concern is not with the essay as an independent document, but as an influence on Pound's method and style, so we will begin with what he had to say about it over a period of about twenty years. First the brief introduction he wrote in 1918:

> We have here not a bare philological discussion, but a study of the fundamentals of all aesthetics. In his search through unknown art Fenollosa, coming upon unknown motives and principles unrecognized in the West, was already led into many modes of thought since fruitful in 'new' Western painting and poetry. He was a forerunner without knowing it and without being known as such.
>
> He discerned principles of writing which he had scarcely time to put into practice. . . .

The accent is still on Fenollosa's relation to art, but already he is beginning to think of him as something more than a mere essayist. The work is 'a study of the fundamentals of all aesthetics'; it deals with new 'modes of thought': the man whose notebooks a few years before had introduced Pound to Chinese poetry, and caused him to write *Cathay,* is now beginning to take on the aspect of a philosopher. By 1933 he *is* a philosopher, one who had outlined the difference between 'the ideogramic method and the medieval or "logical" method'. Here is how Pound explains the 'ideogramic' method in *ABC of Reading:*

> Fenollosa's essay was perhaps too far ahead of his time to be easily comprehended. He did not proclaim his method as a method. He was trying to explain the Chinese ideograph as a means of transmission and registration of thought. He got to the root of the matter, to the root of the difference between what is valid in Chinese thinking and invalid or misleading in a great deal of European thinking and language.
>
> The simplest statement I can make of his meaning is as follows:
>
> In Europe, if you ask a man to define anything, his definition always moves away from the simple things that he knows perfectly well, it recedes into an unknown region, that is a region of remoter and progressively remoter abstraction.
>
> Thus, if you ask him what red is, he says it is a 'colour'.
>
> If you ask him what a colour is, he tells you it is a vibration or a

refraction of light, or a division of the spectrum. . . .

By contrast to the method of abstraction, or of defining things in more and still more general terms, Fenollosa emphasizes the method of science, 'which is the method of poetry', as distinct from that of 'philosophic discussion', and is the way the Chinese go about it in their ideograph or abbreviated picture writing. . . .

But when the Chinaman wanted to make a picture of something more complicated, or of a general idea, how did he go about it?

He is to define red. How can he do it in a picture that isn't painted in red paint?

He puts (or his ancestor put) together the abbreviated pictures of

ROSE   CHERRY
IRON RUST   FLAMINGO

That, you see, is very much the kind of thing a biologist does (in a very much more complicated way) when he gets together a few hundred or thousand slides, and picks out what is necessary for his general state-ment. Something that fits the case, that applies in all of the cases.

The Chinese 'word' or ideogram for red is based on something ev-eryone KNOWS.[1]

In attempting to explain the method further in an article written about 1936, he spoke of 'The clamping of the word to the individual object', which was his aim, or one of his aims, with *Imagisme* in 1912, and then of 'The clamping of word to groups of objects; not necessarily of the same species, that is to say the ideogramic method (for the purpose of poetry)'. And a year later writing *Guide to Kulchur* he renewed his attack on western thought, as distinct from the method of the material sciences. These latter, according to Fenollosa (with whom Pound agreed), 'examined collections of fact, phenomena, specimens, and gathered general equations of real knowledge from them, even though the observed data had no syllogistic connection one with another'. The false knowledge derived from the despised western way of thinking Pound likened to the memorizing of a list of names and maxims from Fiorentino's *History of Philosophy,* and the real knowledge derived by means of the 'ideogramic' method to that of an experienced lover of painting who can tell a picture by Goya from one by Velasquez, and a Velasquez from an Ambrogio Praedis.

To say that this method, as outlined by both Fenollosa and Pound, is built upon a number of misapprehensions is putting it mildly. When Fenollosa wrote of the 'tyranny of medieval logic' from which science had had to break

---

1. It would appear that Pound never actually made enquiries to find out whether the sign for 'red' was in fact made in this way, but believed he had seen it mentioned in Fenollosa. But Fenollosa does not say—not in the essay on the 'Chinese Written Character' at any rate—that the Chinese made the sign for 'red' by putting together the pictures for 'rose, cherry, iron rust, flamingo'. He simply uses the words 'cherry, rose, sunset, iron rust, flamingo' in an explanation of abstract thought, saying nothing at all about Chinese signs.

free, and Pound of the great contrast between the 'method of abstraction' and the 'method of science', they were as far almost from the truth as it is possible to get. Both men harboured the idealistic nineteenth-century view of 'science'. It had a method and if you followed this you got results. Actually this method is composed of at least three separate procedures which play varying parts in the progress of the sciences. There is first the collection of data and accurate labelling; secondly the attempt at describing the behaviour of a selected group of phenomena—this is what people usually mean when they speak of 'scientific method'; and thirdly, the use of imagination, when the scientist, confronted by a problem, some difficulty in current explanations of phenomena, tries to look at it from different angles; and connected with this aspect is the hunch, the guess, the leap ahead, which play a major role in the advancement of science.

Pound and Fenollosa failed to see that science had made such great progress in the western world precisely because it was based upon the European Middle Ages. Galileo, Newton and Einstein all worked from a base built by countless scholars and philosophers of the twelfth, thirteenth, and fourteenth centuries. The idea that the men of the Middle Ages did not examine or even look at phenomena is a sad relic of the Enlightenment; the fact is that they carried out an essential collection and labelling of phenomena upon which our modern science rests. This work was primitive by our present standards, but as A. C. Crombie, lecturer in the History of Science at Oxford, points out in *Augustine to Galileo,* the methods first used with complete maturity by Galileo were expounded in the thirteenth century. There was an essential continuity in the western scientific tradition, from Greek times to the seventeenth century. 'With the recovery of the full tradition of Greek and Arabic science in the twelfth and early thirteenth centuries, and particularly of the works of Aristotle and Euclid, there was born, from the marriage of the empiricism of technics with the rationalism of philosophy and mathematics, a new conscious empirical science seeking to discover the rational structure of nature.' The development of ideas on scientific method, and criticism of the fundamental principles of the thirteenth century system made from the end of the thirteenth to the end of the fifteenth century, prepared the way for the more radical changes of the sixteenth and seventeenth centuries. To a person not trained in modern science, the complexity of medieval science, in its attention to phenomena and precision of method, is quite bewildering, even today.

Working from Fenollosa's mistaken ideas about the history of science, Pound became convinced that modern science had progressed by being in opposition to 'abstract thought', whereas abstract thought is one of the main ingredients in scientific progress. It is because scientists shape and reshape abstractions derived from data that they arrive at new explanations of how phenomena operate. Far from being the process which Pound imagines, modern science moves ahead in its own field because, among other things, scientists have 'logical' thoughts about the material in front of them, no matter how primitive such thoughts may be in comparison with the highly developed thought systems of the Middle Ages. 'In Europe,' says Pound, 'if you ask a man to define anything, his definition always moves away from the simple things that he knows perfectly well, it recedes into an unknown region, that is a region of remoter and progressively remoter abstraction.' Exactly, and it was by juggling with this process that western man created the modern technological world. It was only by working with concepts derived from their data, by going into 'unknown regions', that scientists found new explanations for the processes of limited groups of phenomena. Science, all science, is based upon the assumption that there is 'regularity' in nature and that these regularities may be described in definite terms which will cover all occurrences of the same group of phenomena. It is by abstraction that the scientist draws from some complexity of phenomena a formulation designed to explain how it works. Even Pound's explanation of 'red' depends upon the abstraction of this colour from 'cherry, rose, iron rust, flamingo'. How Pound got the idea that scientists simply heap up information, facts, specimens, and somehow derive knowledge from this material without abstract thought I do not know, but probably it was by his own extension of Fenollosa's ideas in the 'Chinese Written Character'. Unrelated facts or specimens are of no more use to the scientist than to anyone else. What counts is the discovery of relationships and concepts which have a meaning for the scientist, and this implies thought, abstract thought of one kind or another. When Pound speaks of the biologist getting together a hundred or thousand slides and picking out what is necessary for his general statement, he is not, as he seems to think, describing the method of modern science, but only one part of the material technique belonging to one science. Though even this process, as described by Pound, seems to me to imply abstract thought of the western variety, otherwise how is the biologist to arrive at his general statement?

If you think yourself into a position of believing that knowledge, 'real knowledge' to use Pound's term, comes from the mere gathering and examination of objects or facts 'not necessarily of the same species', their examination without 'logical' thought, the final result, if you are a poet or a prose writer, will be the placing together of unrelated things and calling them related for no other reason than that you have placed them together.

Pound's error, I think, was in imagining that the scientist and philosopher indulge in different kinds of thought. Despite the vast differences in the aims and ends of the two disciplines, both use thought, both use 'logical' thought, it is just that the philosopher is much more highly skilled in this department than the other. The progress of the sciences has come mainly through the refinement of techniques, not through any great development of thinking by scientists, but thought is indispensable nevertheless. The reason probably why the two are so often treated as completely different is that people confuse one single aspect of scientific thought—that when the scientist is aware that the facts have outgrown the theory in which they were clothed and is straining to visualize and formulate a new one—with the whole process from beginning to end. The fact is that all human beings who reason do so by means of a

94 NOEL STOCK

process or processes too rapid and subtle for exact description. But to be of any value, reasoning must relate the world of concrete reality with that of abstract notions. As Newman says:

> To apprehend notionally is to have breadth of mind, but to be shallow; to apprehend really is to be deep, but to be narrow-minded. The latter is the conservative principle of knowledge, and the former the principle of its advancement. Without the apprehension of notions, we should forever pace round one small circle of knowledge; without a firm hold upon things, we shall waste ourselves in vague speculations.

Even when reasoning about concrete matters the mind does not merely observe and judge:

> It is plain that formal logical sequence is not in fact the method by which we are enabled to become certain of what is concrete; and it is equally plain what the real and necessary method is. It is the cumulation of probabilities, independent of each other, arising out of the nature and circumstances of the particular case which is under review; probabilities too fine to avail separately, too subtle and circuitous to be convertible into syllogisms, too numerous and various for such conversion, even were they convertible.

The result of Fenollosa's essay was that in the end Pound almost gave up thought altogether, and instead concerned himself with arranging isolated gists, phrases and facts; 'possibly small,' he wrote in 1942, 'but gristly and resilient, that can't be squashed, that insist on being taken into consideration'. And at the end of this trail: the *Thrones* Cantos. There we have isolated phrases, fragments of speech, quotations, facts 'gristly and resilient', all drawn together and related—their only relationship much of the time being that they appear in the same pages together.

From *Poet in Exile: Ezra Pound* (Manchester: Manchester Univ. Press, 1964), pp. 131-42.

DONALD DAVIE

On *Thrones:* Cantos 96-109

IN 1960 Cantos 96 to 109, which had appeared in ones and twos in the magazines, were published together as *Thrones.*[1] *Thrones* got a good press, and this was surprising since even a loyal reader might feel a sinking of the heart as the *Cantos* moved into their second century. Besides, the *Rock-Drill* cantos had seemed in some ways to be foreshadowing a full close to the whole poem. Insofar as the poem had some sort of affinity with the *Divine Comedy* (as Pound had intimated), it had seemed with the *Rock-Drill* cantos that we were moving at last out of Pound's Purgatorio into his Paradiso, since there were passages and whole cantos of an unprecedented serenity, carried in Dantesque imagery of light and flame and the crystal. And it was true that in some of the new group, notably Cantos 102 and 106, the same paradisal quality was clear and haunting. Also it informed and buoyed the Confucian ethics of Canto 99, where the Confucian tradition was distinguished (yet once more) from those other Oriental traditions, Buddhism and the Tao. But Pound much earlier in the poem had jeered at "you who think you will/get through hell in a hurry," and even in *Rock-Drill* it had been clear that the Paradiso was not going to be uniformly paradisal. As for *Thrones,* that title, though it had been foreshadowed in earlier cantos, becomes clearer with Canto 97:

> Mons of Jute should have his name in the record,
> thrones, courage, Mons should have his name in the record.

And when, six lines later, we hear that "When kings quit, the bankers began again," we know what we are in for. We are still going to hear about the iniquities of high finance, which only a monarch can control. And, in fact, we hear about this, not only in Canto 97, but in 96, which is mostly about the disintegration of Rome and the rise of Byzantium; in 100, which deals with European economic history in the eighteenth and nineteenth centuries; in 101, mostly about the American Civil War; and in 107 to 109, which have to do with English history from the standpoint of the great jurists Littleton and especially Coke. It is this last material, much of it quarried from Catherine Drinker Bowen's *The Lion and the Throne,* which is most disquieting, partly

1. Cf. Pound in an interview in *The Paris Review,* 28 (Summer-Fall, 1962), 49: "The thrones in Dante's *Paradiso* are for the spirits of the people who have been responsible for good government. The thrones in the *Cantos* are an attempt to move out from egoism and to establish some definition of an order possible or at any rate conceivable on earth."

because it seems late in the day to have this wholly new field opened up, but
more grievously because some of it is wretchedly written:

> and that slobbering bugger Jim First
> bitched our heritage
> OBIT, in Stratford 1616, Jacques Père obit,
> in 33 years Noll cut down Charlie
> OBIT Coke 1634 & in '49
> Noll cut down Charlie

Elsewhere the old master is still in evidence: as imagiste ("the sky's glass leaded
with elm boughs," Canto 107), as coiner of maxims ("And who try to use the
mind for the senses/drive screws with a hammer"), and, supremely perhaps,
as the paradisal lyrist of controlled synaesthesia:

> stone to stone, as a river descending
> the sound a gemmed light,
> form is from the lute's neck
> (Canto 100)

But no amount of the old accomplishment can make up for the insanely
pointless jocularity of Jim and Noll and Charlie for James I, Cromwell, and
Charles I, or for the Baconian or worse bee that is apparently buzzing in
Pound's bonnet about Shakespeare. In fact, one cannot read *Thrones* without
remembering that the author had spent twelve years in a hospital for the insane.
The best one can do is to remember Christopher Smart's *Rejoice in the Lamb,*
with which *Thrones* has some things pathetically in common, as when a cat,
because it says miaow, is said to "talk . . . with a greek inflection" (Canto 98).
Rejoice in the Lamb, though plainly the product of a mind unhinged, is none
the less a work of genius and somehow a great poem.

From *Ezra Pound: Poet as Sculptor* (New York: Oxford Univ. Press, 1964),
pp. 239-41.

N. CHRISTOPH DE NAGY

Ezra Pound's Poetics

POUND'S DEMANDS concerning poetic diction, besides having considerable importance in themselves, point the way to the centre of his poetics, and, one may add, to the ethics supporting them: the very advice proffered by Pound for the avoidance of *clichés* points back to the supreme function of literature: "The only escape from such is by *precision,* a result of concentrated attention to what is (sic!) writing. The test of a writer is his ability for such concentration AND for his power to stay concentrated till he gets to the end of the poem". For, if this supreme function is, as Pound contends, the "application of word to thing"—"subjective or objective"—i.e. the establishing of adequate connections between the phenomena of the sense world and their interrelations or the facts of psychic life on the one hand and the verbal expressions on the other, the *virtù,* i.e. the highest excellence, of this function will be precision; and if there exist, as is also contended by Pound, universal standards by which all poetry can be evaluated, they, or at least some of them, will perforce be used to determine the degree of precision attained. When the standards are conceptualized to the limit of what Pound seems to think possible, they appear as the principles of composition discussed in this chapter.

If one gathers up, in conclusion, these basic principles, the "norms" that promote the attainment of precision in writing—with the *mot juste* at their centre, as Flaubert himself is at the centre of the "ideograph of the good"—one will in fact see them all to be dependent on the relationship between the "thing" and the word: the permanent "norms", apart from those implied by "scientia", can be reduced to those of the "thing" and the word. From this follows that the writer who aims at representing the world around him—and Pound does not grow tired repeating that "it is very important that there should be clear, unexaggerated, realistic literature"—has first to observe the phenomena of the world with a detached, "impassible" attitude and then to ransack the vocabulary of the language in other to discover the words corresponding to them. How far the writer should draw upon specialized vocabulary, how far he should transcend the immediate impression, what point of view he should choose, are only some of the many problems, all outside the scope of this study, which arise naturally at this point. Flaubert, ploughing through books of chemistry or archaeology before writing his novels, is only to a certain limit a model for Pound: as will be seen in connection with Laforgue, Pound is aware of the exaggerations inherent as a possibility in the very principle of the *mot juste* and existing in certain works of Flaubert as a reality. However, Pound's reservations are secondary: an ultra-specialized vocabulary may simply be unfitting, because it denotes things that have, broadly speaking, no legitimate place in literature; the demand for the subordination of writing to the world outside the poet or writer, this basic "norm", remains.

There is no reference in Pound's critical writings to any Kantian or in particular Schopenhauerian preoccupation with the cognitional basis of the realistic literature that he stipulates; he is inconcerned with the problem of the relationship between the outer "things" and human perception or, by extension, human cognition; there is no reason to suppose that for Pound the world is "recreated" by the "imagination" of the individual. When Pound does deal with a differentiated reaction to the world, he deals with emotional reactions, i.e. personal emotions. In the rendering of personal emotions the "thing" has become "subjective", and the poet has gained greater freedom in his relationship with the outer world, although he draws upon it constantly in symbol and metaphor; the poet alone knows the subjective "thing". The basic norm operating here decisively is language employed according to the principle of the *mot juste* and its implications: the application of this principle entails, as has been shown, a great deal more than merely the labour—sufficiently arduous in itself—of finding the individual *mots justes,* if the uniqueness of the words is to be fully revealed. There exists nothing in the outside world and there is nothing contained in the poet's emotions that it is permissible to render by transgressing the norm of the *mot juste* —which links word to thing.

Pound's central poetics being based on those of theorists and practicioners of prose, most of what has been said on the last pages is applicable equally to prose and poetry. In poetry, however, the musical property of the words will obviously have a stronger effect than in prose, and the degree of precision attainable in poetry will always be conditioned by this fact—by what Pound was to call *melopoeia.*

Altogether, Pound's Flaubertian poetics centred around the *mot juste* had to be adapted to the special needs of poetry, and poetry, as we are often reminded by Pound, is different from prose mainly because of greater concentration. Yet it is not difficult to imagine that a poem written with meticulous adherence to the principle of the *mot juste* may turn out to be heavy and cumbersome. Pound is quite explicit concerning this danger: "The followers of Flaubert deal in exact presentation. They are often so intent on exact presentation that they neglect intensity, selection and concentration". The latter qualities are of particular importance in the rendering of personal emotions, and if Pound wished to get beyond the English poetry of the 19th century, if he wished to cure the specific ills affecting Victorian and post-Victorian poetry, *precision* had to be coupled with *concision.* Pound achieved this by coupling the *mot juste* with the "organic" Image. . . .

Pound's poetics are primarily guidelines helping the poet to find his relationship to the literature of the past and that of his own time; it is a norm of Pound's poetics that such a relationship should be developed in full consciousness and should be based on the assimilated knowledge of the greatest possible number of existing literary forms. Only this knowledge will enable the poet to make an adequate choice regarding the form to be used by him; he may make his choice among preestablished "normative" forms, but they are not binding for him in any way: there is no norm prescribing the use of one particular form rather than another or, generally, the use of an existing form. The poet may, if he feels it imperative, evolve a new "organic" form; but the new form will in some manner be blended with existing ones by any poet who is saturated with the tradition of his art: the new form will likely encompass existing forms.

All poetry, be its form as such "normative" or "organic", has to be subjected to the norms regulating the relationship between the material of poetry and the words expressing it.

From *Ezra Pound's Poetics and Literary Tradition: The Critical Decade* (Bern: Francke Verlag, 1966), pp. 64-66, 86.

HAYDEN CARRUTH

Vision and Style

WHAT IS Pound's vision? It is, all told, extremely complicated as we should expect from so complicated a man. But in essence, like the visions of all great men, it is a vision of goodness, the good that exists somewhere in the universe, the governing excellence at the heart of the world, which is obscured from us most of the time by the imprecision, not to say chaos, of our human arrangements. Pound himself rarely speaks of the good; but more often of equity, order, an honest wage, the importance of ceremonial observances, and the like. In fact, his vision is close to the idealization of human nature that was found on the nineteenth-century American frontier, where Pound was born; it is a pastoral vision, and today it seems almost a trifle quaint—or would if Pound hadn't shaped it in his magnificent style.

Ancient Chinese civilization and particularly the Confucian tradition have been important to Pound for several reasons, but chiefly because he found in them the ideal of a just secular order. On this account he has been accused, by those who miss the point, of mere secularism, which is really preposterous. What Pound is interested in is not secularism but wholeness and union: of spirit and form, mind and body, man and nature. He connects Confucius with many scriptural and mythological counterparts in Asia and the Near East, and with a long line of religious thought in Europe. If these Western connections begin in the temple at Eleusis rather than the temple at Jerusalem, this is not because Pound denies biblical wisdom—that of Abraham or that of Jesus—for he has explicitly affirmed it, but rather because he believes this wisdom to have been distorted and vitiated by the political, economic, and military policies of the church and the Christian rulers. This may or may not have been the case, but it is at least an arguable view, and certainly one held by many historians more exacting than Pound.

Thus Pound's affinities in European civilization have been with Eleusis, the Roman mystery cults, the ritual marriage to the corn goddess, with Gnosticism, the Cabalic tradition, the Albigenses; which in turn connects him with his second consuming passion, the marvelous and heretical literature of the troubadours, or rather the entire development from the Provençal poetry of courtly love, with its close though possibly unconscious paraphrase of Catharist liturgy, to the crowning works of Cavalcanti and Dante. In these areas Pound has made important contributions to scholarship. . . .

Pound alone in our time has created Style—the huge, concrete, multiform artifice that transmits to us the impersonal light beyond art, and from which the artist himself drops away. Pound's best poetry attracts every literate sensibility without reference to temperament or sympathy; it transcends taste. The *Iliad* was written by a man who is a myth, *Hamlet* by a man so uncertain that people spend lifetimes arguing about who and what he was. So with Pound; he is evanescent, and his work—*Personae,* the *Cantos* the translations—stands as fully self-sustaining. If parts of it are boring, is that the unforgivable sin some critics have averred? Of course not. We forgive, gladly, Homer his catalogues and his endlessly repeated epithets, Shakespeare his *Henry VIII* and *Merry Wives.*

Pound well understands the difference between himself and his contemporaries (though his relationship with Williams is more complex than the others). For him it was the difference between Symbolism and Realism, and he chose the latter. Where Yeats and Eliot had looked for an "objective correlative," an image upon which to impress their partial feelings, Pound insisted that the observed detail must stand by itself, an image in the concreteness of its own meaning. Hence his poetry is detailed, and set out in beautifully exact language, for exactness is the key to his sense of beauty.

From "Ezra Pound and the Great Style," *Saturday Review,* 9 April 1966, pp. 21-22, 56.

LOUIS ZUKOFSKY

Ezra Pound: Ta Hio

> Thus, if her colour
> Came against his gaze,
> Tempered as if
> It were through a perfect glaze
>
> He made no immediate application
> Of this to the relation of the state
> To the individual, the month was more temperate
> Because this beauty had been.
>
> 'The Age Demanded,' *Hugh Selwyn Mauberly*

This classifying of values shows Pound sufficiently moral.

For a quarter of a century he has been engaged in 'the expression of an idea of beauty (or order)' and his results are one aspect of a further personal comprehension.

> out of key with his time
> He strove to resuscitate the dead art
> Of poetry; to maintain 'the sublime'
> In the old sense.

—intent upon 'language not petrifying on his hands, preparing for new advances along the lines of true metaphor, that is, interpretative metaphor, or image, as opposed to the ornamental.' 'Artists are the antennae of the race,' words to him are principals of a line of action, a store, a purpose, a retaining of speech and manner, a constant reinterpreting of processes becoming in himself one continuous process, essentially simplification.

He has treated the arts as a science so that their morality and immorality become a matter of accuracy and inaccuracy.

> The arts give us a great percentage of the lasting and unassailable data regarding the nature of man, of immaterial man, of man considered as a thinking and sentient creature. They begin where the science of medicine leaves off or rather they overlap that science. The borders of the two arts overcross.
>
> From medicine we learn that man thrives best when duly washed, aired

and sunned. From the arts we learn that man is whimsical, that one man differs from another.

As there are in medicine the art of diagnosis and the art of cure, so in the arts, so in the particular arts of poetry and of literature, there is the art of diagnosis and there is the art of cure. They call one the cult of ugliness and the other the cult of beauty. Villon, . . . Corbière, . . . Flaubert, . . . diagnosis. Satire, if we are to ride this metaphor to staggers, satire is surgery, insertions and amputations.

In the beginning simple words were enough: Food; water; fire. Both prose and poetry are but an extension of language. Man desires an ever increasingly complicated communication. Gesture serves up to a point. Symbols may serve. When you desire something not present to the eye or when you desire to communicate ideas, you must have recourse to speech. Gradually you wish to communicate something less bare and ambiguous than ideas. You wish to communicate an idea and its modifications, an idea and a crowd of its effects, atmospheres, contradictions. You wish to question whether a certain formula works in every case, or in what percent of cases, etc., etc., etc., you get the Henry James novel.

So that Pound's poetry of music, image and logopoeia, his humanity always the sieve through which the three commute to organic perception, is the same as his personal morality which harbors the clarity of words as well as all beautiful objects, and the peoples who have caused them. And while it harbors their permanence steers through, and around, and is aware of, their temporal situations.

The literary make-up which notices:

> The old swimming hole
> And the boys flopping off the planks
> Or sitting in the underbrush playing mandolins
>
> Canto 13

is inwrapped with the philosophy of Kung, who said:

> Without character you will
> be unable to play on that instrument
> Or to execute the music fit for the Odes.
> The blossoms of the apricot
> blow from the east to the west,
> And I have tried to keep them from falling.
>
> Canto 13

'Character' implies enough order to be radiated outward. Order allows that Kung may permit himself to raise his cane against Yuan Jang,

Yuan Jang being his elder,
For Yuan Jang sat by the roadside pretending to
be receiving wisdom.

                                                          Canto 13

And Kung may also note:

Wang ruled with moderation,
In his day the State was well kept,
And even I can remember
A day when historians left blanks in their writings,
I mean for things they didn't know,
But that time seems to be passing.

                                                          Canto 13

Concern with 'the bright principle of our reason,' with the use of Ta Hio or
The Great Learning as a gauge of action, involves: recognition of the beauty
of everytime in which alone we have being; interest in the present, so that life,
as Pound has said, may not make mock of motion and humans not move as
ossifications.

It follows that Pound has been both the isolated creator and the worldly
pamphleteer. To put the defences of his own being in order, he has drafted
himself into the defence of innovation clarifying and making sincere the
intelligence. Contrasted with the leavings of transcendentalism and belated
scholasticism around him, he has said that 'Lenin invented . . . a new medium,
something between speech and action which is worth . . . study'; (*Exile* 4, 1928)

That the Soviet Idea is as old as the Ta Hio's 'Private gain is not prosperity';

That 'a new language is always said to be obscure . . . After a few years the
difficult passage appears to be a simple lucidity';

That 'perhaps art is healthiest when anonymous . . . in the Grosstadt Symphony we have at last a film that will take serious aesthetic criticism: one that
is in the movement, and that should flatten out the opposition (to Joyce, to
[Pound], to Rodker's *Adolphe*) with steamrolling ease and commodity, not of
course that the authors intended it';

And has implied that Sovkino's *The End of St Petersburg* had an inertia of
mass power behind it impossible of attainment in a single Chekov.

Pound anticipated *The End of St Petersburg* as poetry some years before the
production of the film:

There was a man there talking,
To a thousand, just a short speech, and
Then move 'em on. And he said:
Yes, these people, they are all right, they
Can do everything, everything except act;
And go an' hear 'em, but when they are through
Come to the bolsheviki . . .

And when it broke, there was the crowd there,
And the cossacks, just as always before,
But one thing, the cossacks said:
                    'Pojalouista.'
And that got round in the crowd,
And then a lieutenant of infantry
Ordered 'em to fire into the crowd,
          in the square at the end of the Nevsky,
In front of the Moscow station,
And they wouldn't,
And he pulled his sword on a student for laughing,
And killed him,
And a cossack rode out of his squad
On the other side of the square,
And cut down the lieutenant of infantry
And that was the revolution . . .
          as soon as they named it.
And you can't make 'em,
Nobody knew it was coming. They were all
          ready, the old gang,
Guns on the top of the post-office and the palace,
But none of the leaders knew it was coming.

And there were some killed at the barracks,
But that was between the troops.

                                        Canto 16

That Pound, previous to this presentation, chose to benefit by the clarity
and intelligence of Chinese written character and Confucius is an indication of
the scale he has constructed to measure his values.

Good humor has a great deal to do with this measure. The *Cantos* say
'nothing of the life after death.'

                    Anyone can run to excesses.

                                        Canto 13

Good humor, which is not ashamed to set down fact, has also to do with
Pound's transcriptions of the spoken tongue—his colloquial spelling, and with
exploring music.

From *Prepositions: The Collected Critical Essays of Louis Zukofsky* (New York:
Horizon Press, 1967), pp. 61-65.

E. SAN JUAN, JR.

Ezra Pound's Craftsmanship: An Interpretation of *Hugh Selwyn Mauberley*

CONCEIVED AS a poem with formal parts so unified as to subserve the whole—complete and possessing a certain magnitude—Pound's *Hugh Selwyn Mauberley* reveals its virtues and powers in the style—the devices of representation—by which the poet is able to "imitate" or render in expressive form the subtle, refined workings of a unique sensibility.[1] Our idea of the sensibility to which we attribute the nuances of attitudes and feelings, the antinomies of imaginative logic, articulated in the poem is of course an inference which depends on our grasp of the structure of the poem itself. For Pound, sensibility is a method of transfiguring personae or masks in order to actualize a complex harmony of vision. In *Mauberley*, the speaking voice syncopates in fugal arrangement the splenetic, the maudlin, the serious, and the sublime. Style accordingly conforms in texture and tone—confessional, ironic, pompous, banal—to the shifts of personalities that one will observe as the main cause, the primary rationale, for the intricate variety and the highly allusive, elliptical mode of representation in the poem.

Critical opinion concerning the formal organization of *Mauberley* has in general been diffuse, impressionistic, or ingeniously assured—in any case, unable to define cogently the formal unity of the multiple elements contained within the architectonic rhythm of the whole utterance. While there is agreement about the themes of aesthetic revolt, the polemic of self-justification, and the rhetoric of elegant irony, we still lack a clear and precise elucidation of the organizing principle behind the poem. F. R. Leavis' comments, for example, betray a simplistic opacity: "The poems together form one poem, a representative experience of life—tragedy, comedy, pathos, and irony."[2] In his synoptic gloss, Leavis fails to distinguish the speaker of the first poem from that of the rest. Hugh Kenner, by contrast, is infinitely suggestive about Pound's impersonality: his style is "an effacement of the personal accidents of the perceiving medium in the interests of accurate registration of *moeurs contemporaines.*"[3] But

---

1. Pound's characterization of the poet's sensibility—"persistence of the emotional nature . . . joined with . . . a peculiar sort of control"—invokes Aristotle's "apt use of metaphor" by the poet; see "The Serious Artist," *Literary Essays of Ezra Pound,* ed. T. S. Eliot (London, 1954), p. 52.

2. "Ezra Pound," *Ezra Pound,* ed. Walter Sutton (Englewood Cliffs, N. J., 1963), p. 31; first published in *New Bearings in English Poetry,* 3rd edition (London, 1959), pp. 133-157. See also G. S. Frazer, *Ezra Pound* (Edinburgh, 1960), pp. 53-63.

3. *The Poetry of Ezra Pound* (London, 1951), p. 166.

his actual explication fails to yield the total pattern and orchestration of the various motifs and topics. I suggest that the limitations of modern exegeses of *Mauberley* stem from the approaches and procedures used to determine the informing motivations of the poem by emphasizing language and its symbolic resources to the neglect of the ends or purposes for which language is only a means.

Pound himself demanded a refocusing of attention on the underlying forces that determine poetic structure or, in his terminology, "major form." He implicitly stresses the primacy of ends, controlling intentions, in the creative process:

> Any work of art is a compound of freedom and order. It is perfectly obvious that art hangs between chaos on the one side and mechanics on the other. A pedantic insistence upon detail tends to drive out "major form." A firm hold on major form makes for a freedom of detail. In painting men intent on minutiae gradually lost the sense of form and form-combination. An attempt to restore this sense is branded as "revolution." It is revolution in the philological sense of the term.[4]

By "major form" Pound means exactly the shaping principle which measures and adjusts the possibilities of material and technique toward the realization of an intelligible form. In interpreting *Mauberley,* our concern should be with the kind of action or activity—Aristotle's *praxis* includes doings, thoughts, feelings in dynamic suspension—the poem seeks to present by means appropriate to the attainment of that end.

Our concern, in short, would be with "major form." Explicating the poem on the basis of its organizing principle, of the thematic argument which determines the dialectic interplay of incidents, character, thought, and linguistic properties crystallized in style, we would then formulate the meaning of the poem from the inside, as it were, since our knowledge of what the poet's ends are would tell us by inference the means which he employed to accomplish his ends. These propositions about critical method will make sense only as they show pragmatic efficacy in the process of textual analysis.

Mauberley consists of two parts: the first part, with thirteen sections, projects the negative milieu of the artist by mock-elegy, condensed report, and satiric editorializing; by retrospect, direct monologue, and other means. The concluding poem, "Envoi," may be unquestionably assigned to the persona nearly coinciding with Pound, assuming that the work is partly autobiographical. But I propose that the different personae here be deemed functions of Pound's sensibility; and despite the short-circuiting nexus or asyndetons in syntax and thought, each persona is never exactly equivalent to the poet's mind in its isolation and integral place in the sequence.[5] The totality of the poem may be

---

4. Quoted in T. S. Eliot, *Ezra Pound: His Metric and Poetry* (New York, 1917), p. 15. See also *Literary Essays of Ezra Pound,* pp. 9, 394, 398, 441, and *passim.*

5. Cf. Donald Davie, "Ezra Pound's *Hugh Selwyn Mauberley,*" *The Modern Age,* ed. Boris Ford (Penguin Books, 1964), pp. 318-321.

considered identical with a process of awareness occurring in Pound's mind. In this sense "Envoi" with its rich lyrical cadence affirms a part of the ideal poetic self whose orientation is not toward the Pre-Raphaelite earthly paradise, to recollected scenes in his life, but to the complementing and reconciling possibilities of the future. The address to "dumb-born" (because mutely renouncing) artifice—the bulk of the poem—descants on the *sic transit* idea with triumphant confidence that time and change will prove "Beauty's" immortality.

Like the first poem, presumably E. P.'s "election" or choice of his tomb, "Envoi" confronts the finitude of existence and looks backward, prophetic in adventurousness. But unlike the mock-elegy of the "Ode," which condemns the poet in terms of the past without any hope of appeal, "Envoi" asserts the power of the poet to resurrect the splendid past and reinstate by alchemical magic what time has destroyed in the realm of eternal permanence: "Giving life to the moment,"

> I would bid them live
> As roses might, in magic amber laid,
> Red overwrought with orange and all made
> One substance and one colour
> Braving time.

And the third stanza accepts the future with qualification: "Till change hath broken down / All things save Beauty alone." Within this tight contrastive frame, between the varyingly ironic and pathetic assessment of the poet's heroic aspirations in the "Ode'" and the intimate, cantabile praise of beauty ("her" may refer to integrity, the glorious past, beauty, and England), the ten poems fall in a deliberate sequence whose development leads toward the *peripeteia,* the hypothetical twist, of the "Envoi." In this last section, the poet, cognizing the degenerate times, reverses his fortune by passionately affirming the metempsychosis of experience into vision. The second part of the poem entitled "Mauberley" may be designated as the exploration of conscience, the elaborate plight of identification: the speaker recognizes at last that Mauberley, with his cult of *"l'art pour l'art"* (theory and practice now being delineated in a quasi-narrative manner), has caused his own downfall. "Medallion," the epilogue vindicating his private if passive strength, counterpoints "Envoi" by a successful confrontation of "the face-oval" (the oval being an image of completion or perfection) and a dazzling lucidity transcending the flux of sensual, chaotic experience.

Turning now to the stages of establishing the situation in part one for a character like Mauberley who composes the twelve poems, I would like to trace Pound's ventriloquism—the constant incommensurability of leading motives and surface complexity—as a method of characterizing his persona. In the first poem, as Pound testified, we perceive Mauberley trying to get rid of the poet—a fragment trying to eschew the whole psyche.[6] A certain duplicity, a mixture of

---

6. Thomas E. Connolly, "Further Notes on *Mauberley,*" *Accent* (Winter, 1956), 59: Pound wrote to Connolly: "The worst muddle they [the critics] make is in failing to see that Mauberley buries

condescending praise—"wringing lilies from the acorn"—and restrained, unresolved scorn may be observed in this passage:

> His true Penelope was Flaubert,
> He fished by obstinate isles;
> Observed the elegance of Circe's hair
> Rather than mottoes on sun-dials.

Note the verbs of motivation in context: "strove," "bent resolutely," and "fished," with positive accent laid on the intensive effort giving vital thrust and pressure to the career and poetic vocation which is the object of mourning. Ronsard, Villon, and Flaubert exemplify the creative agents redeeming the apparent failure of the poet to realize the ambition of transforming the tastes of a historical period by cultural discipline. But Pound's death, Mauberley (construing him as the funeral orator) suggests, bears heroic justification. Later the "Envoi's" melodic and delicate speech of farewell will transubstantiate the "Ode's" epigrammatic terseness.

I submit that Mauberley's "juridical" pronouncement on Pound presents an ambiguous "case": he admires and yet censures, by turns lamenting and casuistic. He thus creates a curious "bastard" genre that violates the elegiac form by ramified yet conscientiously accurate and compact descriptions of the ordeals Pound has undergone for the sake of preserving his integrity and his exemplary ideal of cultural engagement. The siren song of surrender and escape to the ivory tower beguiles and chastens at the same time: Circe counsels the pursuit of knowledge when he conveys to Odysseus the importance of communicating with Tiresias, as *Cantos* I and XLVII indicate. Such active passion lurking behind the scrupulous gravity of the poet demonstrates itself in the pure, absolute devotion in the "Envoi" and, by empathy, in the trancelike elevation of "Medallion."

After disclosing his ambivalent but comprehensible attitude to the "dead" and buried self, the whole poet embracing the dualities of self and the world, Mauberley proceeds to place the celebrated figure in relation to his milieu: the "age" demanded exactly the opposite of what Pound intended to achieve. It wanted not "the obscure reveries / Of the inward gaze" but "chiefly a mould in plaster," a mass-manufactured icon for gratifying its narcissistic impulse and death-drive. Poem II identifies the denied offering: the static harmony of truthful, objective synthesis. It accounts also for the futility of the poet's existence: his works "still-born," he becomes useless, later associated with the image of "pickled foetuses."

With a notion of the radical disparity between the poet's conception of the ideal and the epoch's need for "an image / Of its accelerated grimace," Mauberley elaborates on the massive corruption of the body politic and the exorbitant decay of ritual, the commercialized vulgarity of the middle class subverting Attic grace and "ambrosial" Dionysus. The philistine public has

---

E. P. in the first poem: *gets rid of all his troublesome energies."*

ruined tradition, profaned Eros and the mysteries, and annihilated any hope for
a transvaluation of norms:

> All things are a flowing,
> Sage Heracleitus says;
> But a tawdry cheapness
> Shall outlast our days.

The flowing image of reality is fully evoked in Mauberley's drifting and
drowning in the second part. But now Mauberley parodies Pindar's invocation:
instead of bestowing a wreath on Olympic heroes, Mauberley registers the
deplorable decay of honor and virtue in his milieu.[7] Less a jubilant praiser than
a mordant mourner, he criticizes the age in sharply juxtaposed contrasting
imagery. Poem III seeks to assign responsibility for the poet's passage "from
men's memory"—the phrase itself being a non-committal remark. In context,
the passage signifies a temporal and spatial departure in a quest-pilgrimage to
the past, later projected in Mauberley's drift to solipsistic ecstasy in part two.
In cinematic montage, Poems II to XII seek to diagnose the malady and explain
the death of the poet by attributing the cause to the convergence of time and
place to which fate has consigned him.

Poem IV locates corruption and denounces the perversion of ideals embodied
in the sanctity of the homeland by the sacrifice of lives in meaningless mass-
slaughter. The allusions to Cicero and Horace point to the discrepancy between
past and present: the present is witness to the inane confusion of motives, the
desecration of qualities (the fortitude and frankness of youthful combatants)
exacted by the crisis. Hence the age with its fraud and avarice ultimately gets
what it deserves: "laughter out of dead bellies." Yet Mauberley does not
descend into hell (the Homeric motif) simply because he is in hell. He remains
the unflinching if Mephistophelian observer of reality, austerely bitter but not
savagely cynical. Here one discerns an elegiac homage, a truncated bucolic
inspired by Bion, whose intensity is measured by the indignant response to the
visible survivor—in effect, Poem V attacks the equivocal mourner in Poem I
and converts Mauberley from a grudging obituarist to an outraged spirit
instigating revolt by incantatory repetitions—his remedy for the absence of
ritual, Yeats's "custom and ceremony." The balance is restored: the kind of
death acknowledged here, though futile, redeems Pound's "death" from igno-
miny or innocuous obscurity:

> There died a myriad,
> And of the best, among them,
> For an old bitch gone in the teeth,
> For a botched civilization,
> Charm, smiling at the good mouth,

---

7. On the allusion to Pisistratus, see G. Giovannini, "Pound's *Hugh Selwyn Mauberley*, I, iii, 22,"
The Explicator, XVI (March, 1958), Item 35.

Quick eyes gone under earth's lid.

Poems VI to XII, with swift incisive rhythms and sensitive transcriptions, render a plot-like continuum: from retrospective portrayal of the Nineties and the Pre-Raphaelites, then a gradual transit to the present via the interview with Mr. Nixon, a visit to the "stylist," and witty sizing-up of sophisticated females in Poems X and XI. Poem XII ushers us into a drawing-room as setting from which Mauberley launches his tempered indictment of the genteel but debased elite: Lady Valentine's heart seems made up of papier-mâché. On the whole, this section prepares us for Pound's "Envoi" which may be considered as the authentic, noble heritage the dead poet bequeaths to his contemporary apologist-arbiter Mauberley. Clarification of this movement will further disclose the probability of the "Envoi" appearing at this point in the sequence as an eloquent reversal of what the "age" would expect despite the hostile tenor of the previous forensic quatrains.

Yet Mauberley's true sympathy—for the dead Pound (a persona within the poem), not for society—chooses the last two stanzas of Poem XII as the epiphanic contact between the soul and its paradisal repose: the Augustan poise of Dr. Johnson's culture. Charting the sordid plight of the artists from "Yeux Glauques" up to the "stylist" cultivating his own garden so to speak, Mauberley nonetheless halts that merciless, self-chastising exposure of the artist's vanity in order to pay sincere tribute to the dead poet—his real total self—by evoking "Pierian roses" and introducing the matrix of music-flower-love motifs which integrate the second part.

Poems VI to IX present concrete dramatic situations in stylized patterns, the persons and their surroundings contrived to illustrate those who compromised with the age and those who persisted in intransigent defiance. These scenes also serve to distill emotions recollected in tranquil review affording sardonic and aphoristic violence of notation. Spiritual discipline is exercised in achieving balance, a "perspective by incongruity" yielding comic innuendo, as for instance: Lionel Johnson's "pure mind / Arose toward Newman as the whiskey warmed" or "Dowson found harlots cheaper than hotels."

In Poems IV and V, the demands of the age receive exaggerated and abusive response in the loss of innocence and potentiality, a cataclysmic holocaust reducing all human purpose into dust. A reversal of the idea that piety and mores always prevail occurs here. Mauberley painstakingly discovers in disillusionment the vain delusive cause which mocks the value of sacrifice and deprives life of all sacramental import. To withdraw into memory seems the only alternative out of the impasse (later merging into "apathein," impassivity), the intractable mood of nihilism, in Poem V. With "Yeux Glauques," Mauberley strives to resurrect those "quick eyes" swallowed by war's ruins.

Poem VI incorporates in the figure of the female victim the larger scheme of transformation in the whole poem.[8] The Muse here becomes a prostitute:

8. The metamorphic symbolism of *Mauberley,* its "primary pigment," may derive from the Glaucus myth and the parable of the bewitched lover, as suggested by George Knox, "Glaucus

art, represented by Ruskin, Swinburne and the Pre-Raphaelites, has already entered its dying phase at the apotheosis of the pandering bourgeoisie. For the puritanical prudes of Victorian England, beauty smacked of obscene pagan deviations:

> Foetid Buchanan lifted up his voice
> When that faun's head of hers
> Became a pastime for
> Painters and adulterers.

Yet Burne-Jones's painting, levelling the ranks of king and beggar-maid, has ably transfixed an orgiastic moment which defies mutability and fashionable canons of taste. Now, however, the beautiful features of the Pre-Raphaelite model (Elizabeth Siddal) seem artificially fragile, destitute: "Thin like brook-water, / With a vacant gaze." Her luminous eyes still search for a sympathetic or possessive gaze, such as the mesmerized Mauberley's in "Medallion." But there, of course, the rapturous vision explodes so powerfully as to dissolve the firm, "suave bounding-line" and immediately impose self-transcendence. Despite the oppressive indifference of the audience, Mauberley preserves a suspicious distance and reveals the fidelity and sincerity of art in the person of an animated fiction. Thus the persona Mauberley energizes another persona, Jenny the pure unfortunate, liberating the aesthetic vision from the stasis of memory and incarnating its presence in the vivifying context of secular betrayal:

> The thin, clear gaze, the same
> Still darts out faunlike from the half-ruin'd face,
> Questing and passive. . . .
> "Ah, poor Jenny's case" . . .
>
> Bewildered that a world
> Shows no surprise
> At her last maquero's
> Adulteries.

Indignant but cautious, aware of the great propensity for sentimentalism in his subject, Mauberley handles language with ascetic and economical finesse. He does not really believe that Jenny's status is hopeless and beyond rectification. His tone and mode of representing her decline obviously deride the age for its hypocritical rectitude; amidst all indignities, Jenny's beauty remains unblemished, radiant. The pathos of her situation assumes allegorical significance in the quotation heading Poem VII: in Dante's Purgatory, Pia de' Tolomei's flat statement of birth- and death-place attests to a possible salvaging of which Pound's "Envoi" is the prophetic affirmation.

---

in Hugh Selwyn Mauberley," *English Studies*, XLV (1964), 236-237.

Poem VII resumes the elegiac but detached, condensed critique of a hermetic aestheticism founded on Flaubert's code of *le mot juste* and the anti-bourgeois policy of the French Symbolistes.[9] If eunuchs and maqueros ruin the vital erotic union between man and woman (by extension, between artists and the Muse), they also disrupt the continuity of a viable tradition. Paralyzing deracination afflicts Verog's existence:

> Among the pickled foetuses and bottled bones,
> Engaged in perfecting the catalogue,
> I found the last scion of the
> Senatorial families of Strasbourg, Monsieur Verog.

In a recollection within the framework of nostalgic recall, Verog imparts information about the last days of the Rhymers: Dowson's dissipation, Lionel Johnson's fall, etc. His reminiscences, refracted through splintered immediacies of detail, give proof of the arbitrary, shifting *modus vivendi* that the Nineties adopted amidst universal anarchy and disorder. Lumping Bacchus, Terpsichore and the Church, they pursued a Paterian goal of attaining organic beatitude. Intoxicated by alcohol and hashish, Dowson succumbed to his "artificial paradise"; in part two, Mauberley sails toward his occult mirage, an island of spices, but drowns in the process. Aesthetics, exemplified by Pound's assimilation of "influences," appears to be the only hope for restoring a sacramental ambience to the industrial, dehumanized atmosphere of the years circa World War I. With the public's rejection of the "inward gaze," we find Mauberley defining the estranged distinction of the gentleman-scholar:

> M. Verog, out of step with the decade,
> Detached from his contemporaries,
> Neglected by the young,
> Because of these reveries.

Where Poem VII conveyed Mauberley's imitation of Verog's conversation, the next poem "Brennbaum" renders with impressionistic vigor the countenance of a ludicrous "clerk," or connoisseur-intellectual. Infantile and lugubrious stiffness in conformity with orthodox norms blights Brennbaum "The Impeccable." His subservience to the rule of prudence and punctilio undermines memory and repudiates genealogy. Thus Brennbaum appears as Mauberley's nemesis in so far as Brennbaum represents the futility of looking backward, the vapid past signified by his ignoring Mt. Horeb (life-renewing water gushing from the rock) and Sinai, and the mechanical efficiency of mere formal correctness:

9. For a description of the biographical circumstances and the literary sources of the poem, the most useful study is John U. Espey, *Ezra Pound's Mauberley* (Berkeley and Los Angeles, 1955).

> The skylike limpid eyes,
> The circular infant's face,
> The stiffness from spats to collar
> Never relaxing into grace;
>
> The heavy memories of Horeb, Sinai and the forty years,
> Showed only when the daylight fell
> Level across the face
> Of Brennbaum "The Impeccable."

Mauberley's act of describing what is basically the studied shape of a cadaver, anticipated by the preceding "pickled foetuses and bottled bones," constitutes a severe epitaph for Brennbaum. Contrasting with the eulogistic overtones of Poem I, "Brennbaum" factually states what is left of a human being. Anesthetized by empty decorum, Brennbaum's substance reflects his unhonored origin and the tenebrous exodus and liberation of the tribe left unheeded by his public self.

Another case of a death-in-life existence is dramatized in Poem IX, where Mr. Nixon advises compromise in a smugly opportunistic expertise. Selfish Mr. Nixon, however, is seriously limited by his surroundings; he looms as the anti-Odysseus (a composite of worldly, complacent citizens) who negates all the values Mauberley upholds in his twin role of ironist and annalist:

> "I never mentioned a man but with the view
> "Of selling my own works.
> "The tip's a good one, as for literature
> "It gives no man a sinecure.
>
> "And no one knows, at sight, a masterpiece.
> "And give up verse, my boy,
> "There's nothing in it."

Mr. Nixon's coaxing and proverbial rhetoric, though ultimately intended to purge suicidal ambitions, aims to persuade Mauberley to sacrifice his life for the glory of the bitch goddess Success. Mauberley, however, recalls Bloughram and the anti-pastoral equations and imperatives of Victorian evangelists. He recalls the aesthetes whose deaths burlesque those of the soldiers in Poems IV and V. The Rhymers and the Pre-Raphaelites served a spiritual ideal—"the thin, clear gaze" of Venus in her temporal revelations—that was once immanent but is now hardly perceptible.

The next three poems attempt to effect a re-incarnation of beauty (Venus) in a female figure only to end in the resigned news that the sale of "half-hose" has superseded the appreciation of art in the city. As an answer to Mr. Nixon's double-edged program—to save one's life by violating one's integrity—Mauberley allies himself with the impoverished "stylist" who has retreated to the country. But Poem X is not less ambiguous, no more pro- or anti-art, as the first poem if one notes the allowance of positive gifts to the "stylist" and recognizes his incapacity to conduct a harmonious transaction or rapport with his society. Nonetheless, his talent and gusto flourish by coalescing with nature's self-renewing life:

> Nature receives him;
> With a placid and uneducated mistress
> He exercises his talents
> And the soil meets his distress.
>
> The haven from sophistications and contentions
> Leaks through its thatch;
> He offers succulent cooking;
> The door has a creaking latch.

But what then is the "placid and uneducated mistress" doing if the stylist manages household affairs? The next two poems show Mauberley's discriminating insight into the fate of art as personified by female personages or acquaintances.

By the evidence of Poem X, Mauberley conceives of Nature as generous and patronizing, set beside which the stylist's companion is an ineffectual mistress. Certainly it is difficult to envisage this mistress as one of the metamorphosed forms of Sappho or Penelope, let alone Circe. Yet she is one of the representatives of the generative, erotic force in *Mauberley*. Although the house is wretchedly falling apart, the stylist is happy and at peace with his environment. If his proper function is to observe "the elegance of Circe's hair" like Pound's in Poem I, then he is temporarily defunct. But Circe is concealed nowhere; the fault is not his, perhaps. In Poem XI, Mauberley hardly suspects the wife-mistress of "the most bank-clerkly of Englishmen" to be one of her profane re-incarnations. In "habits of mind and feeling," she scarcely evokes the fabled seductiveness of the archetypal goddess. To call her "Conservatrix of Milesien" would be an insinuating joke if not forthright anachronism; her "tea-gown" and her alliance with the commercial class betoken her low pedigree.

In Poem XII, Mauberley projects himself in a drawing-room where amid the insipid and pretentious crowd he suffers an eclipsed consciousness:

> "Daphne with her thighs in bark
> Stretches toward me her leafy hands,"—
> Subjectively. In the stuffed-satin drawing-room
> I await The Lady Valentine's commands,
>
> Knowing my coat has never been
> Of precisely the fashion
> To stimulate, in her,
> A durable passion;

(Note the repeated "bass" beat of aesthetic stasis in frozen Daphne/laurel tree, "tin wreath" of Poem III, metallic flowers, pickled foetuses, porcelain images, etc.) Mauberley experiences an illusory triumph: he imagines Daphne the legendary nymph stretching out a laurelled crown. But that happens "Subjectively," he bravely confesses. In truth he apprehends his actual circumstance with self-deprecatory reference to his non-dandiacal appearance, his nondescript clothes being a natural consequence of his loathing for frills or fustian:

> Doubtful, somewhat, of the value
> Of well-gowned approbation
> Of literary effort,
> But never of The Lady Valentine's vocation:

Mauberley sees the Lady Valentine as a powerful authority who, like Circe, can accomplish her sinister designs by exploiting the thaumaturgy of art. Lady Valentine also functions here as mock-Muse to the poet-Pierrot (Petrushka in Stravinsky's ballet). Defensive and shrewdly realistic, Mauberley would seize this opportunity for his own advancement: for promoting a dubious liaison or ingratiating himself into theater business. Throughout the sequence, Mauberley's sexual prowess is sublimated into Latin ribaldry and etymological punning—as Espey has shown—to fulfill Venus' mandate. In revolution or in any emergency, Lady Valentine would be a refuge, a possible "comforter." Mauberley's physical self as free agent accepts the circumscribed realm of action imposed by a degenerate milieu. But if he can perceive the possibility of living in another manner—the stylist and the dead Pound of the "Ode" offer alternatives—it is because he has a virile spirit capable of epic dignity and tragic purposiveness, a spirit which does not share the mood of resigned futility and his later castrating numbness, nor participate in the body's commitments. Yet his "soul" sent on a journey to an Augustan haven of the imagination only intensifies his awareness that such a haven cannot be found anywhere today:

> Conduct, on the other hand, the soul
> "Which the highest cultures have nourished"
> To Fleet St. where
> Dr. Johnson flourished;
>
> Beside this thoroughfare
> The sale of half-hose has
> Long since superseded the cultivation
> Of Pierian roses.

We encountered this "ubi sunt" motif before in Poem III where we learned that the discordant "pianola" has overthrown Sappho's lure. Cheap imitations flood the market. Nourishment of sensibility is succeeded by "macerations"; the memory of Dr. Johnson's (like Lionel Johnson's) career receives the discounting pun in "Fleet Street"—for fleeting time spoils the genuine artifice and dissolves sensations into phantasmagoria—as part two exhibits. Perhaps the anatomical connotation of "half-hose" escapes the diffident but restrained Mauberley. He forgets the ubiquity of those roses in the "tea-rose" of Poem III; his temperament favors only the precious, rarefied luxuries: "The thin, clear gaze, the same / Still darts out faunlike from the half-ruin'd face." Contrast further Pieria, seat of the worship of the Muses, with Ealing where the lady curator of Milesian ware languishes in chill respectability.

Comparing the amorous "Envoi" and the chiselled strophes of the first part, we note that except for the change in cadence and texture there exists between them a unity of focus on an idealized past (Mauberley celebrated the Pre-Raphaelite model; Pound casts his challenging valedictory in Waller's mold) and in a dualistic notion of existence as comprised by perishable flesh and undying spirit, the spirit able to preserve in art the lineaments of fleshly beauty. Two or three lines uttered by Mauberley may be orchestrated with the climactic bravura of "Envoi":

> The thin, clear gaze, the same
> Still darts out faunlike from the half-ruin'd face,
> Questing and passive . . .
> (Poem VI)

> "Daphne with her thighs in bark
> "Stretches toward me her leafy hands,"—
> (Poem XII)

> Young blood and high blood,
> Fair cheeks, and fine bodies;
> (Poem IV)

The thirteenth poem, instead of enacting a disproof of Mauberley's sentiments, offers him a finely-controlled modulation into Pound's voice.[10] It is as if the poet, whose death occasioned the memorial in Poem I, were resuscitated by the enigmatic verbal magic of Poems II to XII—both the dissonant and the mellifluous—while Mauberley, in speculative and abstracted vigil over his corpse, muses on the whys and wherefores of the artist's ordeal in this mercantile, inimical world. Can one then plausibly construe the "Envoi" as the envoy/embassy of Pound (the dead poet's ghost) speaking with the oracular gestures of hindsight and foresight?[11]

---

10. In "The Modulating Voice of *Hugh Selwyn Mauberley*," *Wisconsin Studies in Contemporary Literature*, VI (Winter-Spring, 1965), 73-96, William V. Spanos argues that the "disjointed nature of the sequence" is dramatically appropriate, but he exposes the weakness of his argument by resorting to the principle of "imitative form." Nowhere has he formulated the meaning of the poem, much less the *mythos* or "action" which defines the organizing principle of *Mauberley*.

11. On *Mauberley's* lack of unity, cf. George Dekker, *Sailing After Knowledge: The Cantos of Ezra Pound* (London, 1963), pp. 154-166. An example of a fallacious verbal analysis of the poem which

In the second part entitled "Mauberley," Pound vigorously turns the tables over and maneuvers the situation so that Mauberley assumes the role of partisan and accomplice, an alter ego with his flawed consciousness. In a condensed and telescoped summation of Mauberley's struggles, this second part modifies and enhances by specific demonstration the attitudes supporting the manner of expression in the first part. Messalina, her licentious urge curbed by her rigorously defined head, supplants Circe; Mauberley, to the speaker Pound (tagged here as the persona), also regards Flaubert "His true Penelope." Kins or brothers by elective affinity, Mauberley and Pound share many interests in common. But Mauberley is distinguished by the kind of art-form he has chosen to concentrate on (announced in Poem I):

> Firmness,
> Not the full smile,
> His art, but an art
> In profile;

The laconic characterization hits the bull's-eye: Mauberley himself has fearfully turned sideways and avoided the full gaze of the female sex: Lady Valentine, the "Conservatrix," and the stylist's mistress. With his satiric craft, however, he was able to depict Brennbaum's countenance: "The skylike limpid eyes, / The circular infant's face"—but then Brennbaum turned out to be a frigid corpse. After Poem II where he indirectly refuses to indulge the age's egocentric delight in beholding its grimace, he is stunned by the impact of war's grotesque testimony: "Charm, smiling at the good mouth, / Quick eyes gone under earth's lid" (Poem V of part one). Brutalized by the ignoble present, he recoils to the past and for a moment he can contemplate directly not Circe's hair but the Pre-Raphaelite nymph, her eyes "Thin like brook-water, / With a vacant gaze." And he records his sympathy and sad impotence in yoking polished loveliness and carnal corruption together:

> The thin, clear gaze, the same
> Still darts out faunlike from the half-ruin'd face,
> Questing and passive. . . .
> "Ah, poor Jenny's case" . . .

This inclination to retreat into an idealized past and witness amid insidious decay the last desperate gasp of the adored Muse (an eclipsed Medusa/Circe/Venus type) seems to have caused Mauberley's "anaesthesis" and his slow disintegration in cosmic nirvana. Poems II, III, and IV in the second part relate

---

evaluates the function of details by initially denying the validity of Pound's structural method and his controlling principles, is A. L. French, "Olympian *Apathein:* Pound's *Hugh Selwyn Mauberley* and Modern Poetry," *Essays in Criticism,* XV (October, 1956), 428-445; see the rejoinder by Christopher Reiss, "In Defence of *Mauberley,*" *Essays in Criticism,* XVI (July, 1966), 351-355, and French's reply in the same issue, pages 356-359.

the progressive extinction of Mauberley's spirit. The epigraph at the head of Poem II, signed by Caid Ali (Pound masquerading as a persona stepping out of an exotic Oriental utopia, or out of the *Rubaiyat*), functions as Pound's flamboyant tribute to his moribund proxy. If Mauberley's passion is too mystical as to be incomprehensible to ordinary mortals, then—Caid Ali (Pound's persona within a persona) implies—whatever feeling or attitude we may have toward Mauberley's earthly vicissitudes will fail to correspond with the real worth of the motives or purposes that have governed his spirit. Fatality has "translated" Mauberley into the empyrean of dreamy necessity, somewhat analogous to Baudelaire's artificial paradise (duly authenticated in *Canto* LXXVI):

> For three years, diabolus in the scale,
> He drank ambrosia,
> All passes, ANANGKE prevails,
> Came end, at last, to that Arcadia.
>
> He had moved amid her phantasmagoria,
> Amid her galaxies,
> NUKTIS 'AGALMA

Is beauty then a deceitful and traumatic hallucination? The experience is valid nonetheless as an example of what "the obscure reveries / Of the inward gaze" can generate. Drifting away from time, Mauberley with his "orchid" as the possessed grail finally reaches "the final estrangement." The erotic associations of orchid-iris-mouth-eyes cluster of images combine with allusions to Hesper, Arcadia, flamingo, thunder, etc., to produce a consistent unifying theme of Eros-in-action throughout the poem. Indeed, the mandate of Eros requires Mauberley's introspective recollection and subtle conjuring: for instance, the perception of "The thin, clear gaze." Obeying such a mandate, he becomes "inconscient" to the phenomena of normal life. He does not need a "sieve" to sift beauty from chaos—in "Envoi," Pound described the "siftings on siftings in oblivion" as ultimately a refining technique. What Mauberley needs is a "seismograph," an inner equipment, fit for his experiment whereby *aesthesis* evolves into "anaesthesis":

> —Given that is his "fundamental passion,"
> This urge to convey the relation
> Of eye-lid and cheek-bone
> By verbal manifestations;
>
> To present the series
> Of curious heads in medallion—

Mauberley as engraver concerns himself with anatomy. Somehow his knowledge or technique fails to reconcile "eye-lid and cheek-bone"—objective perception—with "aerial flowers," his "orchid": organic sensations, physiological vibrations. Thus Pound's oblique judgment of the simultaneous victory and defeat of his enterprise is foregrounded in an Ovidian tableau:

> Mouths biting empty air,
> The still stone dogs,
> Caught in metamorphosis, were
> Left him as epilogues.

Transfixed in this posture, the dogs accompanying the hunt (see *Metamorphoses*, VII, 786ff.) are freed from their violent biological urge. Yet such freedom manifests the impotence, the vitiating inability, of mere animal existence to satisfy man's infinite desires.

Poem III centers on Mauberley's rejection of the age's demands, thus confirming his sympathy for Pound the dead persona-poet in the "Ode." Chance found Mauberley and his unctuous vanity unfit for fulfilling any civic responsibility: his mind is all focused on "The glow of porcelain," the vibrant color of his model's beauty reflected in "a perfect glaze," a translucent veil: to him "the month was more temperate / Because this beauty had been." Inner mood dictates outer climate. But just as in Poem XII in part one, Mauberley suffers from a worsening imbalance: his will to inhabit Arcadia heightens the conflict between *Anangke* and the "manifest universe" and his confessed "diastasis" (separation) from all life, ignoring the erotic or sexual ("The wide-banded irides / And botticellian sprays."). His psychic malady is suggested:

> The coral isle, the lion-coloured sand
> Burst in upon the porcelain revery:
> Impetuous troubling
> Of his imagery.

Exclusion of everything alien to his sensibility induces "the imaginary / Audition of the phantasmal sea-surge," linking up with the earlier signal of "Minoan undulation . . . amid ambrosial circumstances." "Olympian *apathein*" postulates the antithesis to Dionysian celebration and loss of self which accompanies creation; art as icon mediates between the spiritual and the sensual, mobilizing knowledge into action. The deterioration of Mauberley's ego increases with the coagulated sounds of the polysyllabic diction toward the close of Poem III:

> Incapable of the least utterance or composition,
> Emendation, conservation of the "better tradition,"
> Refinement of medium, elimination of superfluities,
> August attraction or concentration.

In spite of Pound's sensitive appreciation of Mauberley's delirious union with deity ("subjective hossanah") in the context of a depraved world, he maintains ironic distance throughout with fastidious quotation marks and subdued parodic touches in such phrases as "insubstantial manna," in sly idiom or parenthetical asides.

Poem IV represents Mauberley's death by the metaphoric vehicle of an aborted voyage cursed and waylaid by the constellation of Hesperus (Beauty). Elpenor's image, the voluptuary aspect of the heroic Odysseus, hovers over the last stanza which discharges Mauberley's barren epitaph on a defunct oar:

> "I was
> "And I no more exist;
> "Here drifted
> "An hedonist."

With "consciousness disjunct," Mauberley attains a kind of supernatural insight into transcendence with the vividly pigmented landscape of his tropic paradise. Associations with Daphne, rose, water, Pindar's wreath, aereal flowers, faun's flesh, oar and foam substantiate the regenerative implications of Mauberley's last glimpses of the world, a world half-dreamt and half-real:

> Thick foliage
> Placid beneath warm suns,
> Tawn fore-shores
> Washed in the cobalt of oblivions;
>
> Or through dawn-mist
> The grey and rose
> Of the juridical
> Flamingoes;

The grey and rose flamingoes seem to render a judgment on Mauberley's struggles, a verdict cancelling the drowning utterance of the "hedonist" inscribed on a drifting oar. But just as Poems II to XII of the first part delivered over the poet's corpse, miraculously revived the poet so that he could sing his "Envoi," so here Poems I to IV succeed in effect, summoning the spirit of the drowned Mauberley back to life in order to recite "Medallion," his true "epilogue" and his humble "adjunct to the Muses' diadem."

Conceived as an epitaph as well as a last will and testament, "Medallion" aptly illuminates the surface complexity, the overall pattern, of the poem. The principle of coherence in the poem lies in the process involving the transfiguration of Venus Anadyomene's face, seen in a reproduction, into a dazzling vision. The depth of Mauberley's inward gaze has succeeded in embodying beauty in a medium perfectly indivisible with the content of his intuition: the verbal medallion redeems the second part just as "Envoi" redeems the whole of the poem. Plunged in "porcelain revery," Mauberley insulates himself against the "profane intrusions" of the blasphemous hollow world. Avoiding direct confrontation with reality, Mauberley sought only the profile; but now nature, in her guise of Anadyomene the goddess of fertility and love, forces him to look straight and recognize that art draws its energy and life-enhancing *virtù* (the emphasis on light accords with Pound's concept of paradise in the later *Cantos*) from the erotic experience itself which lies at the core of the imagination.

In his essay on "Cavalcanti," Pound writes: "The Greek aesthetic would seem to consist wholly in plastic, or in plastic moving toward coitus. . . . "[12] That truth Mauberley has sought to obscure by pure aestheticism and timorous pride, but now this truth asserts itself. "Medallion" embodies this slow awakening into the mystery, the artifact becoming a vessel of the sublime:

> The sleek head emerges
> From the gold-yellow frock
> As Anadyomene in the opening
> Pages of Reinach.
>
> Honey-red, closing the face-oval,
> A basket-work of braids which seem as if they were
> Spun in King Minos' hall
> From metal, or intractable amber;
>
> The face-oval beneath the glaze,
> Bright in its suave bounding-line, as,
> Beneath half-watt rays,
> The eyes turn topaz.

(Note the affinity between the "Envoi's" "in magic amber laid" and the phrase "intractable amber" in "Medallion.") All the other disgraced female personages in the poem, in particular the Pre-Raphaelite Muse with her "clear gaze," merge with the oval face and luminous eyes of sea-borne Aphrodite (Anadyomene: literally, "birth foam"). "Topaz," usually transparent yellowish mineral, continues and amplifies "glaucous eyes" of the Muse-Siddall-Jenny-harlot constellation in the first part. The Sirens, Circe, Penelope, Messalina, Venus, and the courted virgin in "Envoi" (Circe's hair finds analogue in the "basket-work of braids" in "Medallion") blend into the radiant image of Venus arrested yet hauntingly moving in Mauberley's verbal artifice. The poetic "Medallion" then provides a foundation in experience and myth for the dominant action symbolized in the two parts of the whole poem.

For the action imitated by *Mauberley* is essentially the tragic experience of death metaphoric and literal after the loss of psychic equilibrium, conducing to an inquiry by turns comic, satiric, serious, and detached, into motives and ideals in the context of a civilization which has victimized the bearers of the life-sustaining vision of mystery. Poem I states the death of the clairvoyant poet; Poems II to XII survey past and present to define Mauberley's anger,

---

12. *Make It New* (New Haven, 1935), p. 346. See Clark Emery, *Ideas Into Action* (Coral Gables, Florida: Univ. of Miami Press, 1958), pp. 5, 29, 125.

doubts, and despair. Poem XIII, a lyrical affirmation of the spirit, may have inspired Mauberley's "Medallion" since both poems dramatize metamorphosis and exaltation by art. Poems I to IV in the second part recount Mauberley's fortunes, with a reversal effected in "Medallion."

Celebrating the symbolic death and rebirth through art of two poets in a reflexive mode, the whole sequence of *Mauberley* may be seen from one point of view as an extended epitaph to the tombstone of art at a specific time and place: England circa 1918-20. Exorcising demonic skepticism, it functions as a cathartic consolation for the speaker-elegist whose technique, resisting the temptations of the lotus-life ascribed to the exiled Mauberley as well as to the successful literati, changes completely our expectations of the conventional elegy by its problematic orientation. Although the power of nature and pagan cults determine the sympathetic response of the speaker to the poet's predicament, the manner of elucidating death alternately depends on the human resources of rhetoric, calculated irony, recollection, music, intuitive learning, insights, etc.—in short, the complete ensemble of faculties harnessed against the human condition of finitude and contingency. Oscillating between the polarities of "faun's flesh" and "saint's vision," the whole poem evolves as a new species of "ode," neither Pindaric nor Horatian; at first subverting the sublime and elegiac, then developing into a sustained counterpoint between past and present in order to resolve the tension of the predicament (bondage by Circe/art) in the first poem. After showing how civilization drives men to senseless death in war and hinting the prospect of a bleak future, Mauberley is left with no other choice but to seek refuge in the pathetic relics of memory. If he acquiesces to a mediating position in Poem XII, he still implicitly subscribes to the premise of a sharp disparity between, say, neo-classic urbanity and the vulgar materialism of the present.

With "Envoi," Pound himself shifts the modality of expression to pure lyrical assertion of art's transcending life. In the second part of the poem, such a transcendence is projected as immanent in Mauberley's "porcelain revery" which fuses vision and artifice together. The second part functions as the validating framework of the first part, for here Mauberley's character is drawn in terms of his behavior, his decisions, which are needed to clarify his utterance of Poems I to XII of the first part. Pound traces Mauberley's career after the first part has furnished us by suggestion and implication all we want to know (from Mauberley himself) of his "contacts" or crucial experiences, his thoughts and feelings about them. It remains for the poet to give an objective accounting, a graphic résumé, of Mauberley's endeavors to pursue his vocation amidst the perils of the market and the drawing room. But he would not remain for long in society: the exile-death wish motif is announced in the poem's epigraph, a quotation from Eclogue IV of Nemesianus, a counterpart to the sportsman-scholar of the *Rubaiyat.*

Withdrawing from any profound involvement with the issues of his age, Mauberley proceeds to commit the error of the inveterate pleasure-seeker: he elevates the means—sensual experience—into an end. He therefore condemns himself to exhaustion, abandoning the aesthetic imperative of justifying his

124   E. SAN JUAN, JR.

own thoughts and feelings. Paradoxically, sensuality leads to "anaesthesis"; but this detachment does not yield any knowledge or insight of an informing purpose—except "Medallion." With "Medallion," his scrupulous indulgence of the senses may be thought redeemed because of his having experienced (for he has been by training and disposition prepared for this and has indeed practically brought it about) an illumination equal to the degree of his devotion and talent. One cannot legitimately expect anything more from Mauberley at this point, given his character and the conditions of his existence. The nature of the action imitated by *Hugh Selwyn Mauberley* is then organized around the idea of life's affirmation by art as achieved in the tragi-comic quest of a hero assuming varied personae—his ethos in the mode of disclosing its formal wholeness—according to the tensions and resolutions of his agonizing, incandescent consciousness.[13]

First publication.

13. From the "archetypal" viewpoint of Northrop Frye, Mauberley-Pound combines the roles of *alazon* and *eiron* in classical drama; see *Anatomy of Criticism* (Princeton, N. J., 1957), pp. 226-228. For the prosodic qualities of the poem, see Edith Sitwell, "Ezra Pound," *Ezra Pound,* ed. Peter Russell (London and New York, 1950), pp. 44-51. While *Mauberley,* as Hugh Kenner pointed out seventeen years ago, may still be virtually unread, the perception of its depth requires a prior grasp of the subsuming pattern, the structure which gives orientation and perspective for such complex details of meaning one may plumb in its depths. This essay is an attempt to define the formal structure of the poem.

SELECTED BIBLIOGRAPHY

Works of Ezra Pound

A Lume Spento. Venice: A. Antonini, 1908.

Personae of Ezra Pound. London: Elkin Mathews, 1909.

Exultations of Ezra Pound. London: Elkin Mathews, 1909.

The Spirit of Romance. London: Dent, 1910.

Provença: Poems Selected from Personae, Exultations and Canzoniere of Ezra Pound. Boston: Small, Maynard, 1910.

Canzoni of Ezra Pound. London: Elkin Mathews, 1911.

The Ripostes of Ezra Pound Whereunto Are Appended the Complete Poetical Works of T. E. Hulme, with Prefatory Note. London: Swift, 1912.

Noh, or Accomplishment: A Study of the Classical Stage of Japan. With Ernest Fenollosa. 1916; rpt. New York: Knopf, 1917.

Gaudier-Brzeska: A Memoir. 1916; rpt. New York: New Directions, 1960.

Certain Noble Plays of Japan: From the Manuscripts of Ernest Fenollosa. Chosen and finished by Ezra Pound. Churchtown, Dundrum: Cuala Press, 1916; rpt. in *Classic Noh Theatre of Japan.* New York: New Directions, 1959.

Lustra of Ezra Pound. 1916; rpt. New York: Knopf, 1917.

Pavannes and Divagations. 1918; rpt. New York: New Directions, 1958.

Instigations. New York: Boni and Liveright, 1920. Contains Ernest Fenollosa's *The Chinese Written Character as a Medium for Poetry* edited by Pound.

A Draft of XVI Cantos of Ezra Pound. Paris: Three Mountains Press, 1925.

Personae: The Collected Poems of Ezra Pound. 1926; rpt. with additional poems New York: New Directions, 1949.

Antheil: And The Treatise on Harmony. Chicago: Covici, 1927.

Imaginary Letters. Paris: Black Sun Press, 1930.

ABC of Reading. 1934; rpt. Norfolk, Conn.: New Directions, 1951.

Make It New. New Haven: Yale Univ. Press, 1935.

Jefferson and/or Mussolini. 1935; rpt. New York: Liveright, 1936.

Polite Essays. 1937; rpt. Norfolk, Conn.: New Directions, 1939.

Guide to Kulchur. 1938; rpt. as *Culture* Norfolk, Conn.: New Directions, 1938.

Confucius: The Great Digest and The Unwobbling Pivot. Trans. Ezra Pound. 1947; rpt. with Chinese text New York: New Directions, 1951.

The Pisan Cantos. New York: New Directions, 1948.

The Cantos of Ezra Pound. New York: New Directions, 1948. Cantos 1-71 and 74-84.

The Selected Poems of Ezra Pound. New York: New Directions, 1949.

Section: Rock-Drill: 85-95 de los cantares. New York: New Directions, 1949.

Money Pamphlets. 6 vols. London: Peter Russell, 1950-52.

The Letters of Ezra Pound: 1907-1941. Ed. D. D. Paige. New York: Harcourt Brace Jovanovich, 1950.

Patria Mia. Chicago: R. F. Seymour, 1950.

The Translations of Ezra Pound. Ed. Hugh Kenner. 1954; enlarged edition New York: New Directions, 1963.

Literary Essays. Ed. T. S. Eliot. New York: New Directions, 1954.

Shih Ching: The Classic Anthology Defined by Confucius. Cambridge: Harvard Univ. Press, 1954.

Women of Trachis by Sophocles. Trans. Ezra Pound. London: Neville Spearman, 1956.

Thrones: 96-109 de los cantares. New York: New Directions, 1959.

Impact: Essays on Ignorance and the Decline of American Civilization. Chicago: Regnery, 1960.

Love Poems of Ancient Egypt. Trans. Ezra Pound and Noel Stock. New York: New Directions, 1962.

Confucius to Cummings: An Anthology of Poetry. Ed. Ezra Pound and Marcella Spann. New York: New Directions, 1964.

Pound/Joyce: The Letters of Ezra Pound to James Joyce. With Pound's Critical Essays and Articles about Joyce. Ed. Forrest Read. New York: New Directions, 1967.

Bibliographical Aids

Edwards, John, and William Vasse, eds. *Annotated Index to the Cantos of Ezra Pound.* Berkeley: Univ. of California Press, 1957.

Gallup, Donald. *A Bibliography of Ezra Pound.* London: Rupert Hart-Davis, 1963.

Interviews

Bridson, D. G. "An Interview with Ezra Pound." *New Directions 17.* Norfolk, Conn.: New Directions, 1961.

Hall, Donald. "The Art of Poetry V: Ezra Pound." *The Paris Review,* 28 (Summer-Fall, 1962), 22-51.

General Critical and Biographical Studies

Agenda: Ezra Pound Number, 4 (October-November 1965).

Amdur, A. S. *The Poetry of Ezra Pound.* Cambridge: Radcliffe Honors Thesis in English, No. 5, 1936.

Baumann, Walter. *The Rose in the Steel Dust: An Examination of the Cantos of Ezra Pound.* Coral Gables, Fla.: Univ. of Miami Press, 1970.

Carruth, Hayden. "The Poetry of Ezra Pound." *Perspectives 16* (Summer 1956), 129-59.

Cornell, Julien D., ed. *The Trial of Ezra Pound.* New York: J. Day Co., 1966.

Creeley, Robert. "A Note Followed by a Selection of Letters from Ezra Pound." *Agenda,* 4 (October-November 1965), 11-21.

Davenport, Guy. "The Perpendicular Honeycomb: Pound, De Gourmont, Frobenius." *Meanjin,* 14 (December 1955), 492-501.

Davie, Donald. *Ezra Pound: Poet as Sculptor.* New York: Oxford Univ. Press, 1964.

Davis, Earle. *Vision Fugitive: Ezra Pound and Economics.* Lawrence: Univ. Press of Kansas, 1968.

Dekker, George. *Sailing After Knowledge: The Cantos of Ezra Pound.* London: Routledge, Kegan Paul, 1963.

Dembo, L. S. *The Confucian Odes of Ezra Pound.* Berkeley: Univ. of California Press, 1963.

Edwards, John H., ed. *The Pound Newsletter.* Berkeley: Univ. of California, 1954-56. See Number 10, April 1956, for index to series.

Eliot, T. S. "Ezra Pound." *Poetry,* 68 (September 1946), 326-38.

Eliot, T. S. *Ezra Pound, His Metric and Poetry.* 1917; rpt. in *To Criticize the Critic,* New York: Farrar, Straus and Giroux, 1965.

Eliot, T. S. "The Method of Mr. Pound." *The Athenaeum,* 24 October 1919, pp. 1065-66.

Eliot, T. S. "Isolated Superiority." *Dial,* 84 (January 1928), 4-7.

Elliott, George P. "On Pound—Poet of Many Voices." *Carleton Miscellany,* 2 (Summer 1961), 79-103.

Emery, Clark. *Ideas into Action: A Study of Pound's Cantos.* Coral Gables, Fla.: Univ. of Miami Press, 1958.

Espey, John. *Ezra Pound's Mauberley: A Study in Composition.* Berkeley: Univ. of California Press, 1955.

Fraser, G. S. *Ezra Pound.* 1960; rpt. New York: Grove Press, 1961.

Goodwin, K. L. *The Influence of Ezra Pound.* London: Oxford Univ. Press, 1966.

Hesse, Eva, ed. *New Approaches to Ezra Pound.* Berkeley: Univ. of California Press, 1969.

Hutchins, Patricia. *Ezra Pound's Kensington.* London: Faber, 1965.

Jackson, Thomas H. *The Early Poetry of Ezra Pound.* Cambridge: Harvard Univ. Press, 1968.

Kenner, Hugh. *The Poetry of Ezra Pound.* 1951; Norfolk, Conn.: New Directions, 1951.

Leary, Lewis, ed. *Motive and Method in the Cantos of Ezra Pound.* New York: Columbia Univ. Press, 1954.

Mayo, Robert, ed. *The Analyst.* Evanston, Ill.: Northwestern Univ. Department of English, 1953- . Mimeographed publication appearing at intervals, prepared by various hands.

Meacham, Harry M. *The Caged Panther: Ezra Pound at Saint Elizabeths.* New York: Twayne Publishers, Inc., 1967.

Mullins, Eustace. *This Difficult Individual, Ezra Pound.* New York: Fleet, 1961.

Nagy, N. Christoph de. *The Poetry of Ezra Pound: The Pre-Imagist Stage.* Bern: Franke Verlag, 1960.

Nagy, N. Christoph de. *Ezra Pound's Poetics and Literary Tradition.* Bern: Francke Verlag, 1966.

Norman, Charles. *The Case of Ezra Pound.* 1948; rpt. New York: Funk and Wagnalls, 1968.

Norman, Charles. *Ezra Pound.* New York: Macmillan, 1960.

O'Connor, William Van. *Ezra Pound.* Minneapolis: Univ. of Minnesota Press, 1963.

O'Connor, William Van, and Edward Stone, eds. *A Casebook on Ezra Pound.* New York: Crowell, 1959.

Pearlman, Daniel D. *The Barb of Time: On the Unity of Ezra Pound's Cantos.* New York: Oxford Univ. Press, 1969.

Quarterly Review of Literature, Ezra Pound Issue. Vol. 5, no. 2 (1949).

Reck, Michael. *Ezra Pound: A Close-up.* New York: McGraw-Hill, 1967.

Rosenthal, M. L. *The Modern Poets.* New York: Oxford Univ. Press, 1960.

Rosenthal, M. L. *A Primer of Ezra Pound.* New York: Macmillan, 1960.

Russell, Peter, ed. *Ezra Pound: A Collection of Essays to be Presented to Ezra Pound on His Sixty-Fifth Birthday.* London: Peter Nevill, 1950. Published in America as *An Examination of Ezra Pound,* Norfolk, Conn.: New Directions, 1950.

Ruthven, K. K. *Guide to Ezra Pound's Personae (1926).* Berkeley: Univ. of California Press, 1969.

Schneidau, Herbert N. *Ezra Pound: The Image and the Real.* Baton Rouge: Louisiana State Univ. Press, 1965.

Stock, Noel, ed. *Ezra Pound: Perspectives.* Chicago: Regnery, 1965.

Stock, Noel. *Poet in Exile: Ezra Pound.* Manchester: Manchester Univ. Press, 1964.

Stock, Noel. *Reading the Cantos: A Study of Meaning in Ezra Pound.* New York: Pantheon, 1967.

Sullivan, J. P. *Ezra Pound and Sextus Propertius: A Study in Creative Translation.* Austin: Univ. of Texas Press, 1964.

Sutton, Walter, ed. *Ezra Pound: A Collection of Critical Essays.* Englewood Cliffs, N. J.: Prentice-Hall, 1963.

Viereck, Peter. "Pure Poetry, Impure Politics, and Ezra Pound." *Commentary,* 12 (April 1951), 340-46.

Watts, Harold H. *Ezra Pound and the Cantos.* Chicago: Regnery, 1952.

Witemeyer, H. *The Poetry of Ezra Pound: Forms and Renewal, 1908-1920.* Berkeley: Univ. of California Press, 1969.

Yale Literary Magazine: Ezra Pound Number, 126 (December 1958).

Yeats, William Butler. *A Packet for Ezra Pound.* 1929; rpt. in *A Vision,* London: Macmillan, 1937.

Yip, Wai-lim. *Ezra Pound's Cathay.* Princeton: Princeton Univ. Press, 1969.

Zukofsky, Louis. "The Cantos of Ezra Pound." *The Criterion,* 10 (April 1931), 424-40.